What Readers Are Saying About

fear: a spiritual navigation

"I thank God for writers like Jo Kadlecek. By telling the messy truth about her own struggle with fear, she gave me courage to do the same. So go ahead—jump in the deep end. You'll find every graceful word of Jo's to be a life preserver and a helping hand."

—CHARLIE PEACOCK, musician and author of *At the Crossroads*

"Jo Kadlecek's book is a tender tribute to human hold-back. By opening wide the windows of her heart, she urges us out of our own prisons and into the freedom that faith promises."

—ELISA MORGAN, president and CEO of MOPS International

"This book is serious surgery. Jo Kadlecek's transparency in opening up some grievous old wounds is salutary. In this powerful narrative she encourages each of us to face our fears and work with God to realize his grace and transformation in our own lives."

—LUCI SHAW, writer-in-residence at Regent College and author of *Water My Soul* and *The Angles of Light*

"It is wonderfully ironic that a book about fear should be this brave and that this kind of unflinching—even brutal—honesty should produce such a healing, life-giving work. Whatever fears may bind us, Jo Kadlecek has given us a beautiful reminder (or perhaps a revelation) that the Truth really *can* set us free."

—CAROLYN ARENDS, recording artist and author of *Living the Questions*

"A beautifully honest treasure map."

—KELLY MONROE, editor of *Finding God at Harvard*,
founder and director of the Veritas Forum

"Jo's stories combine lofty quotes with gritty, ordinary moments to urge you to keep working through, moving forward, and overcoming when it would be easier to sit it out."

—JAN JOHNSON, author of *When the Soul Listens* and *Enjoying the Presence of God*

"For anyone who has ever struggled with paralyzing fear, Jo Kadlecek's story offers genuine hope. *fear: a spiritual navigation* is an honest and vulnerable journey into what it means to be alive and human. This book influenced my own life in a profound way."

—JOY ROULIER SAWYER, author of *Dancing to the Heartbeat of Redemption* and *The Art of the Soul*

"Jo Kadlecek has found a way in a Buechner-esque writing style, with the authority of a Paul Brand, to explore the anatomy of fear from a personal and spiritual angle. A fine work."

—WES KING, recording artist and musician

"The real trick for writers is to tell their story so that I know my story better. Not many people have the talent to do it or the courage to try. Jo Kadlecek has both."

—ROBERT BENSON, author of *Between the Dreaming and the Coming True* and *Venite*

fear:

A SPIRITUAL NAVIGATION

ALSO BY JO KADLECEK:

Feast of Life: Spiritual Food for Balanced Living

I Call You Friend: Four Women's Stories of Race, Faith, and Friendship
(coauthored with Pamela Toussaint)

*Resurrecting Hope: Powerful Stories of How God Is
Moving to Reach Our Cities*
(coauthored with Dr. John Perkins)

fear:

A SPIRITUAL NAVIGATION

JO KADLECEK

SHAW

WATERBROOK
PRESS

Fear: A Spiritual Navigation
A SHAW BOOK
PUBLISHED BY WATERBROOK PRESS
2375 Telstar Drive, Suite 160
Colorado Springs, CO 80920
A division of Random House, Inc.

Scripture taken from the *Holy Bible, New International Version®*. NIV®. Copyright © 1973, 1978, 1984 by International Bible Society. Used by permission of Zondervan Publishing House. All rights reserved. Also quoted is the *New King James Version.* Copyright © 1982 by Thomas Nelson, Inc. Used by permission. All rights reserved. Scripture quotations also taken from the *King James Version.*

ISBN 0-87788-268-1

Printed in the United States of America
2001—First Edition

10 9 8 7 6 5 4 3 2 1

For my mom and my dad,
who have always believed in me,
even when I was afraid.

contents

acknowledgments

If anyone thinks he can face his fears alone in this world, he is mistaken. Plain and simple. You see, if God himself does not first lean down and whisper in your ear, "Fear not, I am with you," then he disguises himself in another recognizable form: humans. Faces that look you gently in the eye, slip a smile around your tentative soul, and nod to you a certainty that makes you believe you can do this thing, you can face this fear. With some help. You walk together, and that is a divine journey.

Because I know this to be true, I owe an ocean of thanks to those who dared to climb on board with me as I traveled through some scary waters in these pages: To Kathy Houghton, whose honesty about her fears first helped me look at mine; to Laura Grooms, Andrea Clark, Liz Smith, and Joy Sawyer, true friends who read, questioned, and responded to these stories and chapters and then—amazingly—encouraged me to keep writing about these things; to Sue Semrau, whose faithful friendship and open home have always been a light to me; to those who prayed for me throughout the writing process (Pamela, Honja, Daniel, Sandra, Sam, Gloria, Brad, Melissa, Dominic, Melinda, Kristy, Carol); and to my family, of course, for their unending support and patience with me. I would never have left the writing dock, though, had it not been for the vision and thoughtful navigation of my editor and friend, Lil Copan, whose love for language and a good story made it a far easier journey.

Yet it is also true that friends are not the only help you need to navigate these waters; you need a love who "bears all things," who knows when to batten down the hatches for you or when to sit beside you on the deck. My gifted husband stopped what he was doing to read and respond to each chapter as I finished it, brought me flowers, coffee, and kisses on difficult writing days, and continually asked God to have mercy on his wife throughout this exploration.

To him, to my family and friends, and to you, the reader, who might allow my stories of fear and faith to become your own for a few hours, I am grateful. I hope it is a good trip we take together.

Bon voyage.

*"What good is it for a man to gain the whole world,
and yet lose or forfeit his very self?"*

—LUKE 9:25

setting sail

Yes, Crito, that is one fear which you mention,
but by no means the only one.

—SOCRATES

i can't exactly remember the first time I was afraid. Where I
was, what was happening, who was there. I only remember that my
stomach jumped, my palms got sweaty, and I swallowed a lot until
there was not much left to swallow. All of a sudden I felt really wet
under my arms, and my mind jumped around a world of crazy
thoughts. What I also don't remember is if I was four years old or
thirty-four. And it doesn't really matter how old I was because the
feeling was always new, abrupt, paralyzing.

If you have been afraid, you know what I mean, how these four
little letters—f-e-a-r—pry their way into every corner of our lives
and slip into whatever life we happen to be drinking. Most of us
carry a lifetime of fears around with us like we do books, important

papers, or heirlooms; then we move from place to place and find new fears waiting for us when we arrive. Mark Twain was right: "The human race is a race of cowards, and I am not only marching in that procession but carrying a banner."

So being human, it seems to me, is hardly safe. We spend the last couple weeks of summer, for instance, mustering the courage to jump off the high diving board after dreading the deep end of the pool all season. Or we take the first step out of a bad career after years of enduring it. Or we approach God with honest desperation after months of avoiding him. And when we do—that is, when we take a deep breath, stand up tall, and look square into the face of our fear wherever we are—that exhilarating rush of adrenaline that accompanies those moments of abandon and freedom flows through us. It feels good.

But just as all the emotion of our ego is running wild, our fists are firm, our hearts are pounding, reality falls out of the thirteenth-floor window and crashes on our head. We're left staggering on the sidewalk below, holding our banner sideways, shoulders shaking and eyes darting as the whole world passes by. We're relegated—again—to mere mortal status. Cowards.

Our memories are shortsighted. When dealing with fear, we often look for an instant fix. I see now, as a middle-aged woman, my worn path toward security is really a clutter of the how-to books and inspirational tapes I gathered along the way but forgot to apply. They are proof of my attempts to be confident or competent. I get scratched or start to bleed, though, in my efforts to be right or certain or somehow "fixed" of my fears. No matter how I try or what I've accomplished, fear has this habit of waking up with me afresh the morning after I soared through some valiant effort to run my life. Most days, I don't even recognize it as fear. And admittedly, some days are better than others. But that is what fear does: It revisits us soon after we think it is gone. Again and again.

What else does *it* do? Well, I've heard therapists describe fear as "an emotion that occurs when a human or other animal experiences a danger or threat" that manifests itself in particular body sensations: sweating, trembling, increased heart rate, queasiness, tension, and dry mouth. Scientists suggest this fearful sensation happens "from the arousal of the sympathetic branch of the autonomic nervous system, which prepares a body to flee, fight, or 'freeze' when confronted with danger. The hormone epinephrine (adrenaline) is associated with flight and the experience of fear, whereas norepinephrine (noradrenaline) is connected with fight." They say, in other words, that sheep show more epinephrine in their blood and lions more norepinephrine, but any frightened animal can turn and fight when cornered. Maybe that is why pastors or priests suggest fear is simply a spiritual memory lapse, a case of forgetting God loves a human's soul enough to protect her.

Whichever language you or I understand to help us make sense of it, fear does not seem to want to go away. And any honest heart knows the road to facing those "epinephrine hormones" is far from smooth. Navigating such waters is not a one-time task on our to-do list for the day. It is not an all-inclusive, package-deal vacation for one. In fact, I don't think the passage through fear was ever meant to be easy, nor was it meant to be traveled alone. Even when I am afraid and a huge part of me wants to run and hide—alone—it does not take long to see how utterly needy I am for a power grander than my ego, a mind wiser than my own, a compass better than my emotion. And a lot of friends along the way.

Which I suppose is why I have come now to this place. The other part of me—the semi-rational, almost brave part of me—really does want to look at my fears in the light of my faith, hoping that this "exploratory writing" process might move me out of fear's grip and into Another's.

But I have to be honest with you: I never expected to do this so…publicly. In a book, for heaven's sake. For one, I don't feel I have the necessary credentials for writing a book about facing fears: no degree in "phobia confrontation"; no training in anxiety resistance. For two, I do not necessarily enjoy exploring a subject unless I know first that I will attain some level of success.

I am, for instance, somewhat familiar with teaching a college class on, say, how to give a speech or how to write an organized essay. I know what it takes to compose a magazine article or a newsletter profile. And I can—with great certainty, I might add—tell my husband what areas of growth he needs to work on. I also am more than able to recite the Lord's Prayer and sing hymns each Sunday morning at church.

In facing fears, however, I am a novice. A sheep roaming and chomping on a hillside full of weeds and wildflowers, hoping to find something substantial to feed my soul and change my wandering ways. Maybe I'll find it in the questions. Then again, maybe it'll pop out in the stories, in the symbols and tales and prose that describe the journey I am about to share with you.

And maybe this will lead us both to a shore where Truth stands calmly on the sand, extends his hand, and offers to walk beside us through the scary, scary days. That, at least, is my hope.

deep waters

(and the men I almost loved)

I'd rather have roses on my table than diamonds on my neck.

—EMMA GOLDMAN

There are those who say that if you believe in God, there is nothing you should be afraid of. Perhaps that is so. But I have found that the fears themselves have helped me believe all the more in God.

Here is what I mean:

The ocean has always held a strange power over me. Bodies of water, really, have dared me to descend their cool, wet banks ever since I was a little girl.

That in itself is peculiar when you consider where I grew up— in the shadow of Colorado's Rocky Mountains. The foothills, we called them. Virtually within walking distance of forests. Wilderness. Thirteen-thousand-foot peaks. Hiking trails and ski slopes.

The nearest sea splashed on shores more than a thousand miles away, and all I knew were man-made reservoirs, mountain streams, brown lakes, and cement-blue swimming pools.

Still, for some reason, the waters lured me. The freedom of their motion, the mystery of their power—I could not shake their pull.

I suppose I first noticed water before I knew much at all about life. My suburban family belonged to the Monaco Beach and Blade Club, and every summer my older brothers and I walked the two blocks to the club for swimming lessons, swim team practice, or fun in the sun. Aside from the club's winter ice-skating rink (hence, the *Blade* part), Monaco was the landlocked version of what our California cousins enjoyed naturally. We really did have soft beige sand that surrounded a huge circle of water with a concrete slab in the center that we called "The Island." Two low diving boards and a high one in the middle of The Island marked the deep part of the pool, which had a white safety rope surrounding it to keep beginning swimmers—like me—from wandering where they should not go. On the edge of the shallow part where you first got in, eddies were created by little jets of air blowing from the wall that held the water in. The billboard above the gravel parking lot outside claimed that the Monaco Beach and Blade Club had the second-largest swimming pool in the country.

That was fine with me. I loved needling the sand with my toes, paddling through the shallow waters in the pool toward reaching-distance of the white rope, then paddling back, and jumping out of the "kiddy" end exhilarated by my five-year-old accomplishment. I'd skip to where our stuff was, flop belly down on my big, green terry-cloth towel, and watch the water bubbles melt off my arms from the mile-high sun. I stared up and down my little arm muscles at the freckles, the soaked blonde arm hairs becoming dry, and the sand caked on my elbow. As I examined my arms, shivering on the towel the way you do when you first come out of the water, I'd hear the laughter of children, the hollers of mothers, the whistles of lifeguards. Beachballs and sand would land on my towel, but the warmth of the sun tickled my back as if nothing else mattered. Each summer my skin went from pale to red to brown; each summer my hair went from yellow blonde to sun white.

Monaco was my refuge.

Not that I necessarily needed one. By all accounts, ours was a typical middle-class family, enjoying the luxuries of an active suburban life in the 1960s provided by a father who spent most of his time working to make sure he could pay for the luxuries. We looked like most everyone else at the club or in the neighborhood: blonde, pale (or tan, depending on the time of the year), athletic, and...lonely.

I suppose I was only mildly sad that my brothers abandoned me to play Marco Polo with their friends, or that my mother would go play tennis with hers, or that my father would stay long hours at the office. I thought such solitude was normal. So I made the most of sloshing around the shallow end, then digging through the sand and plopping on my towel. Every day. Of every summer of my early years. Alone at Monaco Beach and Blade Club. Kept company by the water in the country's second biggest swimming pool.

To think about it now, I'm grateful for those first times my toes, then ankles, then shins accepted the gentle invitation of the shallow end, thankful for the first feel of sand under my feet, the soothing sun on my back, and mostly, for the way the water gave and took my kicks, giggles, and splashes no matter what happened at home or on the "beach." It was the beginning of a love affair, and I got a crush early on. The big, mysterious liquid arms were kind and fun and tender. They offered comfort when I didn't even know I needed it.

What I also didn't know then was that crushes have a way of sometimes slapping you across the face and laughing at your easy acceptance. No, I was trusting of my water.

Temperatures reached over one hundred degrees one July day, the same day my mother's tennis partners didn't show up. Instead, she decided her daughter's water antics might be entertaining, and the heat certainly gave her a strong incentive to wade with me. I was thrilled. I splashed and held my breath and did headstands, sure she would be pleased with my progress. She stared and murmured politely, "That's nice, honey," though I'm not sure I was compensation for a canceled tennis game.

"Let's swim out to The Island," my mom said suddenly with smug adult confidence. I looked at her tanned face, at The Island, then back again at the woman who had brought me to Monaco in the first place, the woman who faithfully made me peanut butter sandwiches and washed my fluffy towel each week. Was she serious? I could barely paddle to the white rope—splashing was my strong point—how could I possibly survive all the way to The Island?

My mother saw the confusion on her daughter's face and assured me that it would be all right. She held me close as we inched our way to the rope. When she pried my fingers from around her neck and forced them onto the white rope, she told me to hold on tight and it would keep me floating. I didn't have time to protest when she dove under the rope and into the deep end toward The Island. I was stuck. Once I started yelling for mercy, she turned toward me and began treading water halfway between the rope and The Island.

"Well, come on, honey, come out to your mom," she said, blue eyes bobbing up and down. My stomach jumped, almost out of my flesh and into the water. Maybe it was the combination of human support and the familiar liquid comfort that actually made me believe I could do it. Never mind that I really didn't know how to swim yet, that I was still in kiddy lessons. Or that paddling and splashing had not yet gone beyond mere toys of enjoyment to necessary tools of survival. I would try. I would come to my mom, and the water would help me.

But as soon as I let go of the white safety, I swallowed at least a gallon of chlorinated liquid. My coughing turned to panic, and I could neither splash nor paddle. Water came in everywhere, not stroking my shoulders like it had done before, but hurting my lungs, my eyes, my everything. My little tanned arms lunged for anything to help me, but the water showed its force and my mom, for some reason, kept her distance. Anger and pain and confusion exploded in every muscle I had, and I flailed and flapped and writhed with an intensity and verve I did not know I had, perhaps like that of a small cornered sheep who has no choice but to fight a hungry wolf. Why was the water doing this to me? Who was this woman who had coaxed me out of safety and into a terror I had never known before? Where was my mother?

What felt like an hour of hysterical abandon probably ended in five seconds as I felt the firm hand of help grab my waist and pull me back to the rope. The same hand lifted my head out of the water, and staring into my terrified face was another less-terrified one. Tanned, blue eyes no longer bobbing now fixed on my dripping head, and she said, "Well, honey, I guess you *can't* go to The Island." And then she laughed.

My mom then ducked under the rope and swam all the way underwater until she got to The Island. Her head finally bounced out of the water, and still smiling, my mother glanced back at me to make sure I was all right. Then she climbed the ladder onto The Island, walked out onto the low diving board, and dove into the dreaded deep end.

Still trembling from the water's betrayal, I watched my mother swim and climb and dive. Every move she made was graceful, goddesslike, assured. I, on the other hand, was still calming my stomach. Once I collected enough calm to get me out of there, I paddled back to the kiddy's end, sprang out of the pool, and raced toward my towel. I stared hard at the water bubbles melting off my arms, and laid there staring and shaking until it was time to go home.

For the rest of that summer, I did not do much splashing. But I did stay close to the sand and beachballs and terry-cloth towels. As to the big round pool, well, I mostly watched it with a cautious eye. My trust had been broken, so I decided I had better keep my distance from what had once been soothing, attentive, liquid arms.

A phobia is an irrational, obsessive, and intense fear that is focused on a specific circumstance, idea, or thing. Anxiety is an unpleasant emotion characterized by a feeling of vague, unspecified harm. Like fear, it can cause a state of physical disturbance. Evidence exists that some persons may be biochemically vulnerable to an extreme form of anxiety known as "panic attacks."

It is a miracle to me that I am married. It took forty years for me to get to this point, to this place that I thought only other people went. Not that I never appreciated men; no, I rather liked them. Admired them. Noticed them. Their deeper voices, their broader shoulders, their stronger muscles. Like a child watches a lion or a polar bear in a zoo through a glass, safely distant, full of respect.

I feared them.

I suppose it started once I realized they were different. Boys were never much of a big deal to me as a little girl as long as I could play football or hide-and-seek or dodge ball with them. And I could. Equal. As good a quarterback or dodger as any of them. Our neighborhood was lined with as many boys as we had trees, so survival forced me to keep up with them no matter what the game of the day was. No amount of teasing from my brothers could stop me; if anything, their chiding made me all the more determined.

But when our bodies grew and our differences became a little clearer, life—and equality—was not so simple any longer. I'd play dodge ball and be the first kid out because Tommy or Jimmy knocked me down so hard it made me cry. They'd have to stop the dumb game, walk me home, and complain to my mom that I shouldn't have been allowed to play with them in the first place.

"She's a girl! She even acts like a girl!" they'd exclaim to my mother as she sent me to the bathroom to clean myself up. I'd put my hands under the faucet, pat some water on my face, look at the tear-stained face in the mirror, and wonder, *What is so wrong with being a girl?*

Clearly, these boys did not want me around. So I joined the girls' softball team. And I began to read books and write poems in my diary. I started strumming on a Sears plastic guitar, singing

John Denver songs or making up my own. The companionship I found in each of these activities was much more satisfying than getting knocked down in dodge ball. No one complained to my mother about me then, and my father didn't much notice because he was usually still at the office.

By high school, I had gone through a handful of two-week boyfriends. We'd kiss and write notes and pretend to be "close." It made me feel…normal. We'd talk on the phone, and I'd pretend I was popular—until my brothers would run into my room and tell me they couldn't believe *I* had a boyfriend. Who were these guys anyway? Weirdos? Dorks? (Dorks were the precursors of nerds.) None of *their* friends would ever want to date me. Maybe if I lost some weight or got the braces off my teeth, my brothers said, someone cool might be interested in me. Since they both had their pick of girlfriends, I believed they were qualified experts to speak on my love life. I'd look at their cocky blue eyes, hang up the short-lived romances, and retreat to my books and diary, hoping the written words would provide some consolation.

Yes, I believed my brothers. For a long, long time.

By my junior year of high school, I had developed a knack for splashing in the safe places of friendships or clubs or team sports, where my feminine ego would not be threatened or even acknowledged for that matter. Boys had turned into "guys," who seemed to me a good thing to watch but none too good for talkin' to. My relationship with Lee Karns was a good example of how this new tension with clubs, water, and relationships surfaced. He was a senior on the track team, and I found him the perfect specimen of maleness. Tall, tanned, brown eyes, firm muscles, and flashing smile, Lee was beautiful. I'd watch him at track practice as he hurdled or threw the discus with the ease and poise of an Olympian. I watched him as he walked down the halls of our school with confidence and perfection, never a hair out of place, always smiling. I didn't dare talk with him—that would spoil him. So I watched him in the lunchroom, laughing with his track buddies or his cheerleader girl-friends, eating his hamburgers or salads, looking stunning in all his absolute male superiority.

As I came away from my locker one day, preoccupied with homework assignments and fashion insecurities, I almost ran into Lee. How could I not have seen this hunk of male perfection? I fumbled for my books, pretending to be interested in them. I looked around the hall as students hurried to classes, and then an extraordinary thing happened: Lee's brown eyes met mine and he said with great tenderness and depth, "Hi."

I froze. Nothing in my body could be convinced to move; every muscle and nerve ending and joint just shut down. *Biochemically vulnerable.* Anxiety came in everywhere, and though my emotions flailed and writhed for some white rope to grab, my body simply sank in paralysis. My lungs filled up and emptied faster than they ever had. But my eyes stayed fixed on the beautiful face before me, to the "Hi" that now hung in the air bronzed like the words on a trophy. I was numb. Immobile. Dying. Finally, a firm hand of help reached around my waist and directed me to safety.

"Aren't you supposed to be in class, young lady?" It was the vice principal. What seemed to me an hour were four seconds in which the most beautiful guy in the school—maybe the whole world—had acknowledged my existence. He recognized that I was alive. But I had drowned. Thankfully, I was directed toward my classroom. Into safety. Where I could be average. Unnoticed. Sheltered. I sprang out of my fantasy and raced toward English class.

For the rest of my teen years and throughout my twenties, I did not do much guy-watching. Instead, I filled my vision and my life with so many activities that I did not have time for the opposite sex. They, I concluded, were only a distraction, and I had important things to do from here on out.

In learning theory, anxiety is seen both as a response to learned cues and as a drive, or motivator, of behavior. Most learning theorists maintain that anxiety is derived from reaction to pain. Anxiety can thus be reduced by removing or avoiding the source or sources of the situations that have produced pain. Avoidance may become firmly established and lead to constricted or bizarre behavior.

"I sat down on the bank above the beach where I had a splendid view around me. Dead indeed is the heart from which the balmy air of the sea cannot banish sorrow and grief." The words the Irish writer Peig Sayers said of her homeland in the 1920s were words I could not appreciate until I had sat a long, long time on the bank above the sea. They were words, though, that have apparently rung true for scores of writers or other poets of life on the pages of their stories or verse throughout literary history. *Water,* for the creative soul, for the spiritually hungry, has served a healthy meal of inspiration—and provision—for hundreds of years. Its kindness, power, mystery, and movement, it seems to me, have not been a thing of horror but rather something to be re-created or "caught" on paper or canvas, something that moved the artist in admiration to a greater truth and freedom.

For me, though, it has mostly meant one thing: terror.

My mother's only brother and sister-in-law lived in Honolulu throughout my childhood, and so during my last year of high school, my father took time off from work at Christmas break and flew our family to visit our relatives in Hawaii for a few weeks. We stayed in their family room, smelling the flowers and fresh tropical plants that grew in their backyard, hearing the tension-filled conversations that hung throughout the two-story house. My uncle was rarely nice to my mother—or anyone else in those days—and so our times in his home were strained attempts at "being family." After a few days with them on this trip, we flew to another island where my dad and mom, two brothers, and I stayed at a fancy resort. Playing tennis. Eating pineapple and shrimp. Swimming in the hotel's pool. And with me staying safely on the beach.

Of course, my brothers would not walk *along* the beach. They wanted the water. They attacked it. They had mastered—as well as landlocked young men could—the art of body surfing, and we could not get them out of the ocean. Catching the waves. Riding the surf. Filling their lungs with enough bragging material to take back home to their friends who had suffered through the Colorado cold of Christmas break. Their bodies got tanned like they did in our Monaco days, their hair sun-white. But I was content enough collecting shells or reading books in the hotel room or playing tennis with my dad on the strange clay courts.

The ocean had not been kind to me before. As a thirteen-year-old, I had experienced the unsettling power of the waves in Mexico, where we had traveled one spring on a business trip with my father. A series of breakers knocked my feet out from under me one morning, only minutes after I had mustered the courage to wade in the water at all. They sent my ankles in two different directions, my arms fighting for anything to hold my balance, and my eyes wide open, smarting from the salt, looking for whatever way was up. I could not tell. Panic punched my belly, but within seconds the water finished its work and dumped me on the shore, facedown in the sand. It retreated just long enough for me to throw my legs beneath me and run toward my family and my towel. That was all the reason I needed not to be tempted now by Hawaii waves.

"You can have them," I proclaimed to my brothers about the waves, as sure and stubborn about remaining away from them as they were about riding them.

Snorkeling in a calm cove on another side of the island, however, was a different story. The popular tourist site seemed harmless enough and only a short walk away from our resort. You could rent flippers there, my mother promised, masks as well as snorkels, and go exploring next to the orange, blue, silver, and yellow fish with stripes and shiny tails that glittered in the sunlight. Besides, the water was barely shoulder high, with only a slight current going in and out of the cove. I listened with seventeen-year-old reason. It was the ocean, yes, but what possible danger could there be in these still, sheltered waters?

I wobbled in with my rubber gear, convincing myself that I was likely to discover a whole new species of fish or coral. *This could be fun,* I mumbled through the tube to no one in particular. Mask glued around my eyes and snorkel fitted tightly in my mouth, I waded to where the water came a little below my neck. I sighed. I looked around at the happy snorkelers, thought about my brothers back in the waves on the other side of the island, and reckoned there was little risk of humiliation here. My mother was lost in a novel on the cove's beach, and my father was playing tennis back at the resort. There were lifeguards on the shore and families everywhere, laughing and fighting and splashing. I watched the sun glistening off the water, palm trees swaying in the breeze on the sand, boats stretching past on the horizon, and little kids gazing at the underworld through purple plastic masks. The water line stayed at my shoulders.

I did everything *but* snorkel. Why? Because during every

attempt to put my nose in the water and kick my fins, I found I could not breathe. Not because the gadget wasn't working; I just could not get enough air. When I *did* keep my face in the water longer than a minute to see schools of yellow and silver and blue swim by me, I'd bite down on the rubber mouthpiece so hard my jaw began to ache. As my eyes would get wider and wider behind the plastic lens, my jaw would clamp down tighter and tighter. And my stomach would flip and jump at just the possibility of something going wrong. *What if these little, slimy water creatures got close enough to actually touch me? What if a tidal wave came? What if a jellyfish stung me? What if the lifeguard didn't see me flopping or flailing if I went under? What if a stupid kid ran into me and knocked me unconscious?* What if…what if…what if?

Avoidance may become firmly established and lead to constricted or bizarre behavior.

My mother was not particularly happy that I was interrupting her beach reading, dripping wet over her, blocking her sun with my strange snorkel-and-mask shadow.

"What's the matter now, honey?" I could not tell her that I could not do it. So I just sat down on the towel beside her, grunted something about too many bratty kids in the water, and threw off the constricting gear. My towel was a soft comfort beneath me as I sat for a long time and stared hard at the bobbing heads in the cove, the boats beyond, and the enormity of the water. Once again it had challenged me and I had lost.

From here on out, I decided, I would live without that which had teased me, slapped me, betrayed me, and downright terrified me. Forget the ocean.

And that's what I did, too, for the next twenty years.

Two types of anxiety are recognized in psychoanalysis. The first, traumatic anxiety, results from overstimulation. Events happen faster than the mind can comprehend them and it produces a feeling of crisis. Freud believed birth throws every child into a state of traumatic anxiety and that this birth trauma becomes the template for later episodes of anxiety. The second type of anxiety, signal anxiety, is believed to arise from a person's need to guard against traumatic anxiety. The ego appraises its ability to cope with external demands and the push of internal drives. When normal methods of coping with these pressures threaten to fail, the ego responds with anxiety, which then mobilizes the person to take new action. A small-scale discomfort of signal anxiety helps to avoid a more devastating experience.

"Fear has a smell, as love does."

— MARGARET ATWOOD

Someone once told me that if a person loses a sense, such as her sight or hearing, her other senses become stronger. She compensates for the loss by developing another sense, one she before might have taken for granted, one which quickly surpasses that of normal human capacity, sort of in the "bionic" realm. For instance, it is not uncommon for a blind woman to be able to smell a flower several yards away. Or for a deaf child to notice much more than what a hearing adult might see. I guess when you do without one part of life, you throw yourself into another.

Love, I knew at the age of thirty from what books, movies, and my friends told me, was a basic requirement around which all the other senses revolved and developed: standard equipment for a human hoping to live a full and meaningful life. Not really similar to junior-high romances or periodic dates or crushes on beautiful people. But a good thing by most accounts, the stuff of poetry and songs and romantic adventures; a sixth sense, if you will, that propels the inherent human need for companionship and affirmation into satisfaction and bliss. It is love that lures the soul away from danger and into a refuge of care; it is love, they said, that gives you a reason to get up in the morning.

So I fell in love. Not the way Hollywood shows you with its steamy scenes and shallow stands. And not even the way my college friends celebrated romance with their boyfriends or husbands. No, I gave my heart away first to a rock called religion and then to a lover called career.

Once I graduated from college, I entered adulthood armed not only with a diploma and a teaching certificate but also with some sense of Christian faith I had picked up in a high-school youth group. I had an inkling as to the right prayers to pray and the appropriate words to "share" with others at church or in ministries. I read the Bible regularly, studied Christian books, and attended worship gatherings or services each week. My diary—which was now a journal—became an ongoing and personal dialogue with the God "who so loved the world that he gave his only begotten son." God was the Creator of heaven and earth, Jesus the answer to any question, the Holy Spirit the guide through every troubled water. More than any other theory or fact I memorized in college, I dove into my twenties really believing the old children's song was true: "Jesus loves me! This I know, for the Bible tells me so."

It wasn't any particular church or spiritual event that taught me this but rather a few people's sincere faith in God and the Bible, which wooed me to my first real experience with love. Jesus cared deeply for my needs, they told me, he affirmed my gifts, he listened when I needed to talk. Then when I discovered from my own reading the accounts of his life, death, and resurrection in the Gospels, I was all the more convinced of who would become the object of my devotion. The gentle Christ, the Prince of Peace, the Savior of sinners had called *me* to come close to his chest and rest in his arms. I was a willing sweetheart.

And I became his champion. From family members and students to colleagues and friends, I talked about this man who walked the earth as God in the flesh to give us love and grace and purpose. My zeal at first was pure, like a child who shows off her newly acquired gift to polite adults.

But loyalty is short-lived when competition elbows its way in.

Teaching became my other passion. A career in education provided meaning and opportunity and confidence. Students *needed* me, and I was determined to be a consistent point of encouragement for them. If I wasn't serving as a faculty adviser for a student Bible study, I was grading papers, coaching the debate team, or preparing lessons that were sure to inspire, equip, and motivate these young people to new heights. Souls would be saved and good would be accomplished. With God's help, I'd tell them, we could do anything.

The truth, of course, was that we could not. That, it seems to me now, is a great American myth I picked up along the road, one that nonchalantly throws God into an already shaky equation created in hopes of attaining a sort of superpower status—an ironic thing indeed, since biblical faith suggests success is found in failure, life in death, and strength in weakness. I had a lot to learn about love.

Nonetheless, these two passions so consumed my life that I shut off the other gifts love tried to offer. Any time a man looked my way, for instance, I'd assume he was either interested in an opportunity to unleash his hormones or in "just being friends," neither of which appealed to me, probably because I was either ashamed of one or afraid of the other. Or if a friend invited me on a vacation or to a social event, I'd dismiss such invitations as petty or a waste of time. They were not as important, not as necessary for the betterment of the world, as my efforts as a Christian teacher.

No one can serve two masters for long before one will eventually prove a tyrant.

By the time I entered my thirties, my heart had been broken and my vision of the world of education skewed. Truth be told, I was exhausted. In addition to confronting my own internal chaos, I could not keep up with the pace of classes, teen emotions, coaching, lesson plans, and extracurricular duties. (I'm absolutely convinced now that lifelong public school teachers are nothing short of heroic!) Worn out from my inability to please two lovers, restless for some sense of peace, I surrendered a career that had demanded more than I could really give and avoided relationships that had asked for more than I knew how to return.

By this point I was empty from having made too many debilitating choices, broken from having failed too many people along the way, reduced to crisis, meltdown. In need of fresh balm. But any doctor will tell you it's easier for a wound to heal if it has first been opened, emptied of infection, and cleansed with a purifying salve.

It was graduate school, a move into an urban neighborhood, and an appointment at a small Christian college in the suburbs that moved me from the open wound into a place where healing began. I started singing "Jesus Loves Me" again. And finally, I was getting some rest.

Then I met Steven. By the time I turned thirty-three—the year of the crucifixion, friends liked to remind me—I was having a full-blown romance with the idea of romance. Fearing men now seemed more of an adolescent approach to life, and I told God I was "open" to the possibility of knowing a man intimately. This was marrying age, and my biological clock was moving on schedule, I was told. Steven, two years older, was a man of intellect, passion, simplicity, and faith. He loved urban life, books, and God. He had grown up a child of missionary parents, spoke French fluently, and now worked as a mental health counselor. "A nice guy," friends and family said. "Perfect for you." I kept my cool, of course, watching, wondering, not daring to hope. And for some reason, Steven could not stop asking me—or everyone else, for that matter—questions. He acknowledged my existence with apparent interest, a willing ear, and a confident sense of romance I had not before experienced.

Wading seemed harmless enough, I told myself.

But within a year, we were engaged to be married. On Cupid's day in February, just after my church's Valentine's banquet, Steven proposed. And for days after that, I walked around in sheer wonder, stunned by the diamond that sparkled off of my finger and into my heart, struck by all that it represented. I was going to be a bride—the ultimate example of femininity. A man wanted me, cared about me, and appreciated me. Maybe my brothers were wrong after all, I thought. For now I enjoyed the gazes from people who simply noticed the normalcy of our togetherness as we walked into a restaurant or a theater. I was not alone. Not self-sufficient. Not just surviving as a single woman. I was engaged.

"When you pass through the waters, I will be with you," God said through the prophet Isaiah.

By the time we were to send out wedding invitations, though, Steven's feet began to wander. My pastor had been counseling us in premarital sessions, and it was clear from those meetings that Steven's expectations were far different from mine. Yes, he wanted to be married, he said to the pastor, and it might as well be to "someone like Jo." As if I weren't even in the room. He explained how he wanted someone who would listen to him upon demand, who would meet all of his needs when he wanted them met. I kept swallowing until I had nothing left to swallow. The more he talked, the more my palms sweated as I realized that behind his constant inquiries into other people's lives, behind the deflecting and "nice-guy" image, was a deeply disappointed man whose disappointment easily—and privately—turned to rage.

The last time I saw Steven he was screaming just inches from my face about how miserable I had made him, how hurt he was that I had not changed enough for him, how selfish and "hyper-spiritual" I had become. I tried hard not to believe him, but I was afraid all over again. I walked out of his apartment shattered, alone, emotions flailing for some sort of safety, confused as to how in the world I had let this happen. Water came in everywhere. The man I thought I would spend my life with continued shouting at me as I stumbled down his steps and into five months of the deepest grief I have known before or since.

When normal methods of coping with these pressures threaten to fail, the ego responds with anxiety, which then mobilizes the person to take new action. A small-scale discomfort of signal anxiety helps to avoid a more devastating experience.

How I wanted to believe at that point in my life that all men were jerks, that their "species" was inherently flawed and, therefore, unredeemable. Forget about them. Who needs them? But my First Love would not let me. Throughout the next year, he plopped not one, not two, but *three* men into my life to become my closest friends (and who had to work pretty hard at it, I might add). Daniel, Linden, and Craig sought me out. Took me fishing in a lake. Cooked my dinner or washed my car. And my brothers began calling—just to talk. Seeing what their little sister was up to these days. Even my once-busy father took time for me, gave me an office in his business to pursue—and affirm—my writing, and took me out to lunch every Friday. Just to be friends. Real friends.

So that's where I thought men would stay from that time on. Just friends.

In studying the control of anxiety, some psychologists focus on the role of cognition as the origin of anxiety. Cognitive theories emphasize the process of appraisal and the often unnoticed

internal dialogue that amplifies emotional response. Experiments have shown that the interpretation of a situation determines whether a person feels anxiety or some other emotion. Learning to substitute benign reappraisals for unrealistically negative "self-talk" reduces anxiety.

If being human is about anything, it is about resilience, survival, the will to live. As created beings, we yearn for opportunities to re-create ourselves, to gather just the right materials to express or reflect a piece of who we are to the world. We seek to contribute our own colors, songs, images, words, or dances. Creativity, I suppose, is the ability to hope through times in the dark, knowing they will not last long, that the broad gracious strokes of change will ultimately bring growth and refreshment. Like rain on hot dry soil. There is a Guinean proverb that says, "He who does not cultivate his field will die of hunger." And I am beginning to believe that is true of the Christian life, which, of course, is inherently creative, instinctively cultivating. Resurrection happens again and again in a person's heart, ensuring that there is no chance ever of starving to death.

It was a strange thing to hear the call of the water again. A complete surprise. I was almost thirty-six years old, still happily landlocked, and now enjoying a solidly single life, teaching part-time to supplement my exploratory writing vocation. The bills were being paid, food was on the table, lights went on in the house, and a few articles got published here and there. Urban life was full and rich. Friends were gathering together with me to build authentic Christian community. I was learning to enjoy my family. And marriage had returned to the secret status of "a nice idea for other people." The game plan did not need changing.

Why I suddenly had this longing for the beach was baffling. I cannot explain it, in mere mortal terms at least. It was more than a craving for sun or a desire for summer exercise, more than a nice vacation plan or a group getaway idea. No, this was an honest-to-goodness longing that actually ached; my soul cried out for it. And I had to listen.

I took every chance I had to get to the shore. (Which was no easy thing for a woman on a limited budget in the Colorado Rockies.) I went to a work-related literary conference in Atlanta and convinced a friend to rent a car with me to drive three hours south to Savannah's beaches. For a few hours at the shore. To hear the ocean drop onto the sand and flow out again. I accepted an editing job in Mississippi, two and a half hours from the Gulf Coast and drove the southern back roads every other weekend to feel the ocean breeze, listen to the waves, or watch the sun turn colors across the water. I took on writing projects close to the Alabama coast or Florida shore, insisting on hotel rooms near the water. I could not get enough.

But I also could not get in. The reunion with the beach was enchanting enough. Why spoil it by getting wet?

When I finally moved to New York City—a place I had long been in love with—I was both wildly ecstatic and quietly relieved to learn that the Long Island Rail Road would take you in an hour from midtown-Manhattan and dump you two blocks from the beach. Long Beach. Wide, white, sandy beaches. Old-fashioned board-walks and lifeguards. Salty water and constant waves. I felt as if I had come home.

If you've ever been to New York in the summer, you know that the sun scorches the sidewalks and makes the whole city seem hundreds of degrees hotter than it really is. The unrelenting coastal humidity hangs over the streets like clouds of tension just waiting to burst; tempers run short every July and August while temperatures run high. Skyscrapers block the blue sky and lush green plant life is hard to come by, except in parks. In many ways, summer in the city is an assault on all your senses, and it is easy to find every reason possible to get to the shore.

Perhaps it was familiarity alone that began to challenge my childhood fears of the water. At first, I'd go weekly with friends to Long Beach or Long Island, watch them swim for hours in the choppy waves while I waved to them from my towel on the sand, and then when the sun set, we'd ride the train back to the city, chattering the whole way about what the water had given us. Maybe it was the rational thinking that sometimes comes with adulthood. But after about the fifth or sixth trip, I no longer could ignore the invitation to wade beyond the ankle-deep water and into the shifting deeper waves. Maybe it was a deeper certainty in the Maker of the sea that had finally begun to take root in my heart. A "benign appraisal" confirmed for me that the benefits outweighed the potential hazards, and one July day I found myself both amazed and relieved (if one can be both at the same time) to be walking toward the Atlantic Ocean, an enormous body of water, that was as welcoming and soothing as I had once—a long time ago—believed it to be.

Slowly, stomach jumping, I exchanged the safety of the terry cloth for the risky change of the tide. "Jesus loves me! This I know," I hummed with deliberate focus as my toes touched the blue-gray water. First my feet, then my shins, then my waist. Before I knew what was really happening, the cool of the water calmed me like a strong arm around a nervous child, soothing the heat and my nerves and encouraging me to stay. It was an innocent caress. So I kicked my feet, splashing like I used to at Monaco. I paddled a bit like I had as a kid. There was freedom in these shallow waves, both exhilarating and peaceful. Soothing, joyous, and safe. I could not stop smiling.

And I could not get out of the water.

Jesus said, "He who believes in me…out of his heart will flow rivers of living water." Something about facing this old fear with a few splashing moments made me feel wondrously alive.

My friend Andrea and I decided by September that the ocean fun should continue and booked one of those spoiled-rotten mini-vacations in Montego Bay, Jamaica. It came after a demanding year of writing projects, and I was ready to relax. She was tired from hard hours in social work among the poor in the Bronx. The idea of resting in the sun by the ocean for five days straight was glorious to us both.

Christian friendship has a nice habit of drawing you out of old selfish ways and into caring for someone else's well-being, loving your neighbor as yourself.

Andrea wanted to snorkel one day. I did not. But now at thirty-eight years old, I figured it was time to take control of my snorkel-phobia and sacrifice my pride for the sake of a good vacation with a good friend. We signed up for the afternoon boat ride, rode the five or so miles from shore, and listened to the ocean stillness as the boat cut its engine. The crew offered each of us the usual snorkeling gear, and without hesitation my friend jumped overboard to begin her aquatic adventure. She was an exemplary athlete, a lover of nature, and a confident woman who rarely found a challenge she did not accept. She was in her element.

And I was immersed in snorkeling terror. *It's just a stupid rubber air pipe,* I told myself. *Besides, the fish are more afraid of me than I am of them.* I put on the gear, shivering in the ninety-degree heat, and climbed very slowly down the boat's ladder into the ocean. I sighed, wiped the drip on my forehead, and looked around at the other tourist-snorklers enjoying the colorful underworld story. I treaded water for what felt like hours. In fact, it was probably only about six seconds that passed before inspiration hit, and I realized I had nothing to lose. I ducked my face in the water and began to kick with all my might.

I was not disappointed. There below me were enormous caverns of coral, sunlight beaming down like thick bright arms, schools of beautiful silver, gold, orange and red fish jetting by, in and out of

the reeds and rocks, long dark green blades swaying slow motion–
like on the water's floor. I clamped down hard on the snorkel's
mouthpiece, still nervous from the reality of what I was doing but
in awe of what I was seeing. I watched long blue fish stroll beneath
me and tiny red fish dart around me, red and white coral ledges
with black holes and mysterious shapes serving as their playground.
I felt the cool salt of the Jamaica sea, the sun caressing my back,
and the indescribable quiet that echoes throughout an underwater
world. Below me was a breathtaking array of God's creative, gracious hand. I sighed a full lung's worth of air. Only occasionally did
I pop my head back up to see the sky or where the others were, but
just as quickly I would plop my face back down, kick my rubber
fins, and circle around the boat, still staring at the marvel below.

"Let everything that has breath praise the Lord," the psalmist
says. I saw praise swimming everywhere that afternoon.

That night I slept with such serenity that I felt I had rested for
weeks. I dreamed blues and greens and yellows, tender movements
of water-hands going over my shoulders, quiet depths stilling my
soul. There was little else that could make me feel so alive, so
human, so loved.

How could I have known then that within the next year, my
water "baptism" would prepare me for a risk greater than diving
into the sea, a love more stirring than the coral reefs of Montego
Bay? Yes, two rivers were coming into the ocean.

The summer after Jamaica, I swam the Long Island waters some
more, laughed with the wind, tried every now and then (when my

confidence was up and the tide was down) to ride the waves. My hair got sun white, and my arms went from pale to red to tan by the time Andrea and I joined friends for an eight-day bicycling trip around Ireland's Dingle Peninsula in late August. (That is another story you will read later.) By early September we were traveling to England—the same week the world was devastated by Princess Diana's death—where I would report on a Christian reconciliation conference for a few U.S. magazines.

I do not know why God would allow an entire world to grieve over the loss of a very human and beautiful princess. And I do not know why God would allow a Colorado girl to find her prince—a man of the sea, no less—that same week, why he would bring two people together from opposite corners of the world.

I only know he did.

The conference photographer was an Australian on assignment with his Christian mission agency. Since my editors told me to include pictures with my articles on the conference, I noticed the Australian photographer—but not only because he was taking pictures. He himself *was* a picture. Sky-blue eyes, firm shoulders, soft heart, and gentle voice. I noticed him, though I was hardly looking to notice. I asked him for some photos, and he agreed. And a few days later we were sharing a stout and a conversation. We talked of literature and justice and growing up in suburbs.

A few months later he came to New York City. We visited Lady Liberty, St. John's Cathedral, the Rockefeller Center, and places in our hearts. And a few years later he became my husband, moving all the way from (where else but a beach?) the Sunshine Coast down under to live near me and marry me. We took a honeymoon near the water, set up a little apartment in the city, argued, rode bicycles, worshiped in church together, talked endlessly, and became better people together than if we had stayed single. Each day is still as adventurous as sailing the sea.

At least, that is my Gettysburg Address version. If you were to ask him, he would give you every *War and Peace* detail. That is part of his passion—and most of the time I love that quality in him. Of course, it was really not as simple or as easy as what I have told you here, because love and courtship and marriage never are. Especially for forty-year-old women who have spent most of their lives avoiding the pain and joy of intimacy. I shall spare you the analysis and fine points (in this chapter), but suffice it to say that from here looking back, I see now that being afraid was more demanding and depleting than the thing itself.

I stepped *back* into the water and discovered a miracle I never expected—but always hoped—to find. Which is why, I suppose, the fears themselves have helped me believe all the more in God.

tender ears

(and the secrets I want to tell)

Oh, be careful—if you breathe, it breaks!

—LAURA, from Tennessee Williams's play *The Glass Menagerie*

a soul that yearns for connection is like glass, it seems to me; even the tiniest movement toward it can be cause for caution. Yet its very nature requires attention, admiration even. Words. Language that calms or invites. And so without a sense of certainty—a spiritual anchor, if you will—this soul wanders through life like a small helpless animal, always on the defensive, alert to any possible threat, starving for some type of rest or connection. It shivers at every sound, even if it is only the wind.

I know this is true.

Our 1967 Ford station wagon was packed each summer with brown sleeping bags, coolers, Coleman lanterns and stoves, and a swimming-pool blue, "family size" deluxe tent. It was an amazing tent, I remember now, with two short side rooms attached to the center space. It must have looked like a ridiculous symbol of suburbia in the midst of the mountain wilderness places where my family went camping. Whether the Colorado Rockies or South Dakota's Black Hills or Wyoming's Yellowstone, the powder blue monster stood up—and out—summer after summer next to evergreens and mountain streams. One-week-long camping trips—suburban style—were a family tradition.

I'm not exactly sure what the point was. Maybe my parents felt some deep burden to expose my brothers and me to the great outdoors, to make sure we knew there was a whole world of trees and rocks and rivers that existed well beyond the trimmed yards and brick houses of our neighborhood. Or maybe they just wanted to get away from the trimmed yards themselves and do some exploring of their own. My father had grown up on a farm in eastern Colorado that had a river running through it, so "being one with nature" was in his blood. My mother, on the other hand, graduated from high school in Alaska but moved so many times as a girl that traveling—not the wilderness—was second nature to her. So the compromise came, I suppose, when my dad could enjoy the scent of pine and forest while my mom could travel with all the comforts of home packed in the back of the station wagon. My brothers loved the adventures, and I went along for the ride.

One summer when I was almost eleven, we headed north to the campground that sat just under the heads of George Washington, Abe Lincoln, and Thomas Jefferson. (Teddy Roosevelt's face was being repaired.) Mount Rushmore seemed a strange place to me—every gift shop we went in, every souvenir stand, every diner, sold more artifacts of Native American culture than of governmental glory. Why, then, I asked my mom, did these presidents' faces get carved in the side of the mountain instead of Indians? Why, in fact, did they mess up the mountain in the first place?

"That's just how they did it, honey," she answered as we hurried back to the blue-monster tent in our campground. My dad had promised to take us fishing one day at the lake a few hundred yards from our tent, so we bought our worms and bait and drove the dirt road toward our site. My brothers got out their skinny fishing poles and walked behind our tall, quiet father toward the water. I grabbed mine and stared at them, then at my mother as she lit the Coleman stove, then back toward the water, not sure which would be worse: standing for hours in the silence of this wide and mysterious lake or staying and helping my mom chop potatoes for potato salad while she chatted with the neighbors from the adjoining campsite. Every other time we had gone camping, my dad had taken us fishing. And each time, we came back to my mother empty-handed. No fish even seemed interested in our bait. What made me think today would be different? Still, adult conversation seemed too difficult to endure, so I rushed toward the lake, pole in hand and anxiety jumping in my stomach.

For the child who is more familiar with street sounds than the crackling of twigs and wild birds, a mountain forest is a daunting creature who can easily swallow up her tiny, lonely life. In a blur, my legs skittered down the haunted trail toward my dad and brothers, and I breathed again when I finally stood next to my father.

He cast his line out over the smooth and glassy water with the same quiet confidence with which he approached most things. My brothers climbed onto huge rocks that sat nearby on the edge of the lake and plopped their lines toward the center. My dad pointed me to a clearing a few yards away where a tree trunk had fallen and now stretched over a shallow part. I obeyed. If I sat right on the edge of the trunk, my feet could touch the water, tickled by the wet swirl whenever I felt brave enough to drop them down. I threw my line toward the center of the shallow part, and I waited.

The hot July sun competed with the mosquitoes to turn patches of my arms red as I sat on the log. I swatted the annoying bugs away while keeping my balance above the water. When this got boring, I'd count the number of birds hovering above me. Occasionally, I'd look around and watch squirrels chasing each other up and down the trees. Then I'd pick off some of the tree's bark, throw it in the water to see if it would float toward my brothers. I looked at them trying hard to catch something, and I looked up at my dad to see the same determined face. So I pressed my eyebrows together, pierced my lips tight, and decided to stare at my pole for the next hour. I could be determined too.

"Hey, Dad, catch anything yet?" I hollered after about a

minute, eager for him to notice my efforts, for any point of contact at all. Maybe he would ask me how I was doing, if I had caught anything or if the sun was too hot for me. Maybe he would invite me over to his rock and ask me to spray his arms with insect repellent. Maybe he'd challenge me to a contest of who could throw bark or stones the farthest into the lake. Maybe he'd even take me into the water for a swim and, like he did sometimes at Monaco, let me hang around his neck so I wouldn't be afraid.

Childhood souls are happy with even the tiniest link to adult security. What might seem like only a slight pat on the shoulder to a forty-year-old is a steadying hand of comfort to a young shivering girl. There is no small interaction for her.

Maybe my dad and I would even catch a fish together.

Instead he turned his head toward me, smiled slightly, looked at me from behind his dark framed glasses, and whispered, "Shhhh, honey, you'll scare the fish!" With that, my throat dried up and my eyes darted toward the crystal water, searching for any sign of life other than green plants. I saw none. I studied the water below me on the right, then on the left, and still saw no movement anywhere. I dropped my feet to see if I could feel anything but cold liquid on my toes, and I pulled them back up quickly when I couldn't.

My dad was right. Apparently the sound of my voice really had scared them off. In fact, because of me, these fish by now were certain we were up there waiting to catch just one of them so we could eat him for dinner. I was sure they had outsmarted us by staying close to the river's base instead of getting hurt.

Self-protection knows no strangers in the animal kingdom. Apparently even fish know better than to tempt the powers that be by disclosing their whereabouts. Little girls are not born with such an instinct; it is learned.

I settled back onto the edge of the tree trunk, pulled my line back in, laid my pole beside me, and waited—strangely cold— until my brothers and father were sufficiently tested before heading back to the campsite. My mom was already grilling hamburgers; somehow she knew that the lake had done to us what it had always done: it refused to give us food for the night. And as far as I can remember, we never did catch a single fish in any lake or river all the summers we went camping.

To communicate, according to dictionaries, is to make known, to transmit to another (as a disease), to give or interchange thoughts or information, to express one's true feelings easily, to receive the Eucharist, or to be joined or connected (as rooms). It is to announce, disclose, reveal, tell. The study of communication is a relatively new field, derived from the academic world of psychology, where experts suggest that the best models involve a circular process. Sender encodes message to receiver, who decodes message and then becomes the sender as he encodes feedback to the sender-receiver to decode again. The process never stops because, they suggest, one cannot *not* communicate.

One of the first arguments my husband and I ever had was long before I knew we would be married. He had come to visit me in New York City for a few October weeks, and after several days of awkward interactions, we went for a bicycle ride around Central Park. The leaves had gone from golden and red to brown and scattered as the crisp fall air slapped our faces, preparing us, it seemed, for a soul-stirring encounter with reality. We passed the reservoir and continued around the park, next to horses and buggies that carried die-hard tourists. In silence, side by side, we pedaled and focused on the road ahead.

When we came to the northern end of the park and hurried past a little waterfall that sits in strange irony across the park road from a huge swimming pool, I decided we should talk. He had been trying to determine whether he should fly back home sooner rather than later, asking for some gauge of where I thought we stood in terms of this relationship. We parked our bikes on the grass next to the Harlem pond, and I pulled up some courage.

"I'm not really sure you're interested in a relationship…with me," I said, looking as far away from this man's face as I could. I stared at the trees, the pond, my black bicycle with the letters *S-p-e-c-i-a-l-i-z-e-d* painted on it in red. I grumbled silently to

God. I watched the white clouds crawl across the blue sky, anything to avoid the vulnerability of eye contact. In my mind it was a fair statement; never mind that this man had flown around the world to visit, changing work plans and fighting personal illness to be with me. The week together had made me question his intentions.

His eyes grew large and his brows pressed with confusion when I finally did catch a glimpse of him before looking away again to safety. *Communication is to express one's true feelings easily, or to be joined or connected, as rooms.* He cleared his throat as my shoulders shivered for a second. The air felt colder.

"How could you say that?" His voice grew desperate in the question as he grabbed a few blades of grass, pulled them from the ground, and tossed them to the wind. Adult confidence was waning. For us both.

"Because it seems you're much more interested in making sure I know about your life and your world than you are in knowing mine," I said with Kadlecek determination. I had lived almost forty years by now and felt I had learned enough about relationships along the way to make my concerns known honestly and quickly, trying hard to help the communication process continue moving. I knew too well that if words and feelings paused somewhere in the cycle, it could be a long, slow wait before anything stirred again. I sincerely wanted to do the right thing, to respond with Christian integrity, regardless of how difficult I thought it might be. Besides, what I had said was true; I could not remember one question he asked me that week about…me—what I thought about this, how I felt about that. I did not recall a single moment when he paused long enough from telling me his own story and opinions to listen to mine.

The leaves rustled around us as children ran past us toward the ducks. I watched an elderly dark-skinned man with white hair throw out his fishing line from the bank of the pond, take a few steps to the side, then reel it back in, only to cast it out again. I wondered if the fish in Central Park hid on the bottom of the lake to avoid the baits that bobbed above them. And suddenly I wondered how I had gotten into this conversation in the first place.

Somewhere on the journey, I had concluded that God had given me only so much time on this planet and therefore every friendship I would have should be one of depth, where listening would be a priority and dignity a respected exchange. I resolved early on in my thinking life not to succumb to what I perceived as superficial banterings about the weather or the latest chatter I had heard on the street. I guess it is true that when you sit in the waiting long enough, eventually you get tired and go looking for something better.

I even went to college to earn my first degree in speech communication and on to graduate school to earn my second degree in cross-cultural communication—probably to make up for the lack of words exchanged in my suburban upbringing. I figured what I lacked in personal training I would make up for in academia, which I hoped would equip me with enough tools to nurture the meaningful relationships I had always longed for. I also made a point of watching a few full-time Christian ministers whom I admired as they interacted with people, noticing how they nodded their heads as they listened and affirmed the person's words with a facial expression that reflected genuine interest. Listening, I had come to believe, was the highest compliment you could pay another human being. Now, the last thing I would allow myself to do was enter into a relationship with a man where I was not heard and, therefore, not known—I had had enough of that in Colorado, where only a few years before a broken engagement had crushed my spirit, an angry fist thrown at crystal.

Intimacy has an alluring power that pulls and pushes a sore heart at the same time.

And so at the edge of the pond, I sat across from this Australian man waiting for words to drop out of my mouth to explain the importance I placed on listening, waiting for all the studied theories and imported language to show him what I meant by knowing and being known by someone. When the words and theories finally did come, I was as surprised as anyone to watch my emotions flying in their midst like fishing lines across water. I sat, argued, attacked, and defended with familiar caution, casting out feelings and reeling them in again. I trembled in the October cold; it was not a pretty exchange.

Apparently, though, it was effective, because what was supposed to have been a two-week visit turned into ten. This man stayed around because, he said, at least he knew where he stood with me, and he appreciated that I would be honest with him. Somehow he came to recognize that my reckless attempts at discussion were reflective of a softer yearning. Now it was *my* brows pressed in confusion at this uncommon combination: a man who craved words. Slowly, astonishingly, the exchange began to steady my soul, though not without first tipping it sideways.

Most psychologists believe that all of us, to some extent, live two lives: an external life, in which we learn the attitudes, feelings, and behaviors that are "safe" to express; and an internal life, in which we closet away our "unsafe" traits, which exist isolated and undeveloped. Sometimes our deep hurts and immaturities have been isolated from relationship for so long that we no longer have access to certain feelings, thoughts, or memories. In this case, hiding is a device used to protect us from overwhelming pain when we aren't ready for it.

I cannot remember many family discussions growing up. I'm sure we had at least a few where we talked about more than who was doing what chores or who had what athletic events to play that week. But for some reason, those deeper conversations have not stayed in my recollections. A friend recently told me she thought that might be because if I didn't talk about an experience as a child, it wasn't entered or processed into my "computerlike" memory to be called up later when I was older. If that is true, I must have been a very subdued child (a conclusion to which I'm sure my mother would object).

I do remember driving back from camping trips and playing three-letter word games in the car or trying to spot license plates from all fifty states. I remember tickling my mom's hand as she rested her arm along the top of the seat and watching her face grow increasingly irritated with my game as she'd swat my fingers as though they were mosquitoes. At restaurants or truck stops along the way home, the conversation always and only turned to who was ordering what meal. But for me the dinner menu was always the same: fried jumbo shrimp with cocktail sauce. Food from the sea. It was a dependable taste, and though I didn't know it at the time, I needed some consistent comfort.

When we returned from our Mount Rushmore camping extravaganza, my brothers and I were enrolled for the rest of the summer in local swim clubs. I had a particularly kind teacher that July. Her brown, wavy, wet hair glistened in the sunlight, and her short height made my peers and me feel tall and, therefore, important. She seemed to care that we learned more than just the back- or breaststroke. She listened to us.

That in itself was a good thing since swim club was far from my favorite pastime; I'd rather have been reading Nancy Drew mysteries or playing first base on our neighborhood girls' softball team. Water's power had pushed me one too many times, and I was not often a willing participant in its games. I could cope being at its edge, sitting on a log or standing near it. But entering its uncertainty without the steady neck of someone older to hold onto quickened my heart rate.

Still, I had to endure the summer activities—swim club would be good for me, my mother told me—and so I went, committed only to learning the backstroke because then my face did not have to be in the water, where I might lose control. I could throw my arms behind me one after the other, kick my toes heavenward, toss my head back, and study the Colorado blue sky.

When I swam, I'd think about everything but swimming or camping or houses where tension hung in the air like storm clouds ready to burst. Besides, my teacher-coach was cheering for me on the other end, encouraging me, calling me by name.

To this day, I am still astounded by the spell an adult's word has over a child: it can be either the foundation that keeps her rooted and safe or the wave that tosses her against the rocks. You know this is true.

So each hot day for the next several weeks, I went to swim club with a belly of mixed emotions, preparing for what our tiny but tender teacher told us would be the best part of the summer: a meet across town at another neighborhood pool. I was not so sure, but I was willing to believe her; she said my name with such kindness.

There would be diving, relays, and individual races in freestyle, breast, butterfly, and back; I would be competing in the backstroke.

When we arrived at the meet, our team eyed the size of the place and realized smugly that we came from a much bigger pool, as if that gave us an advantage. My race was not until the end of the meet, so I could sit in the stands, away from the water, teasing my teammates from a distance. Diving would be first, and one smaller red-haired girl from our team was to go off the low board. It had taken her weeks to find the courage to climb up the ladder, walk out on the board, and make the dive, but today the teacher proclaimed for all of us to hear, she was ready. The young girl could make the dive.

Even now I'm not sure what compelled me to do it: inherent evil, adolescent stupidity, spiritual immaturity, or competition's nerves. Maybe I remembered the time my father threw our dachshunds into the river to "teach 'em to swim," and sure enough, they had paddled back toward him, panting and waving their heads above the water line. I guess I didn't know then that animal lessons did not apply to humans.

Whatever the reason, I slipped off the bench and crept up behind the redhead as she was making her way to the deep end for a few practice dives. Though her pale white skin was still dry from the Colorado sun, I could see that her little freckled shoulders were shaking back and forth. But she walked toward the boards anyway, determination blocking out any noise around her. Just as she was inches from the pool, I pushed out my forearm against her back and gave her a shove that caught her completely off guard. Terror shattered the air as the redhead fell sideways into the deep end, making a remarkable splash for a girl her size. And for the next few seconds, the girl's body went down deeper and deeper. I tossed back my head and chuckled to the sky.

Then water came in everywhere for the young girl, and she wailed and bobbed with a verve she did not know she had. Her arms flew up, then down, while her head popped below and above the water. My sick laughter was instantly silenced as the entire population of Colorado looked our way and saw a panicked redhead in the deep end with an immature blond girl standing above her on the cement. I froze. Next I saw brown, glistening, wavy hair spring into the water, put her arms around the waist of the bobbing girl, and pull her to the metal ladder at the pool's side. Now it was my shoulders that shook as I looked into the face of my coughing, terrified teammate. She spent a few minutes spitting out water, coughing some more, and clinging to the neck of our nice coach, who by now was glaring up at me with a disdain I never imagined she was capable of. Slowly the girl climbed out of the deep end and slowly, cautiously, she stepped far away from me and walked to the stands. She would not dive that day after all.

And I would not swim the backstroke that day, my coach informed me, inches from my face. How could I have done that? she asked in a voice louder than I had ever heard her. Didn't I know how hard she had worked just to get the girl to go off the diving board in the first place? Now it would take a long, long time—if at all—for the young redhead to build up her confidence to try again. Can you even imagine how she is feeling right now?

Well, yes, I could. I shut my eyes and hung my head. The feelings didn't dare come forward.

Shame is a great crippler, lodging words in your throat for a long uneasy time. You turn inward, closeting or isolating your humiliation with such determination that many years later it becomes difficult even to access the memory of what took you there in the first place. Hiding becomes a familiar accomplice.

"I am deeply disappointed in you, Jo," and with that my nice brown-haired swimming teacher walked away from me and toward the bench where the young girl was lying on her terry-cloth towel, belly down, shaking.

I watched both for a long slow hour, until another coach finally told me to sit down, the meet was getting ready to begin. Then my eyes darted back toward the pool. Once again the water had teased me and once again it betrayed me, only this time I was not the only one who had been upset. This time it pushed away the white safety rope of human connection. I had disappointed my coach by shoving the girl into the deep end, and I did not know when—or if—I'd hear her speak my name again. I didn't care at all about races that day, and I was sure I wouldn't come to swim club again.

I cannot remember if I ever spoke about that day with anyone or not, but one thing is sure: The swim meet was *not* the best part of the summer.

"[S]ince it requires the extension of ourselves, love is always either work or courage. If an act is not one of work or courage, then it is not an act of love. The principal form that the work of love takes is attention. When we love another we give him or her our attention; we attend to that person's growth.... The act of attending requires that we make the effort to set aside our existing preoccupations and actively shift our consciousness. Attention is an act of will, of work against the inertia of our minds.... By far the most common and important way in which we can exercise our attention is by listening."

—M. SCOTT PECK, *The Road Less Traveled*

If there is one thing God is particularly good at, it is reminding us that we are not in charge. Try as we may, the values, qualities, and status we work so hard to cultivate really aren't the center of our worlds, no matter how much we might live as if they were. He alone is the Almighty. And mystery, I've come to recognize, is his specialty. When we stand on a shoreline, for instance, staring at a horizon we can't even see, we are strangely comforted. Maybe it is recognizing the truth of our smallness that yields guiding perspective. Maybe it is the ocean's size and secrets that help us remember the protective boundaries that have been set and what could happen if we did not respect them. Though fear of losing control grips most of us, deep in our beings we want nothing more than to admit we never had it in the first place, to know the freedom of a surrendered soul.

We don't sing "How Great Thou Art" on Sundays for nothing.

By February of the next year, the Australian decided he would up and move from his side of the world to mine. He settled into an apartment conveniently located a few floors above me, and during the next five months we had a few more encounters with reality as we went to the theater, attended church services, shared meals and movies, and talked with neighbors. Together. In a relationship. I was hoping for connection, on my terms, in my time; he was hoping for a future.

What happened instead was a lot of button pushing. Emotions long buried were suddenly resurrected in the new life of this thing called *us*. Like two children battling for the same prize, we threw out words with thoughtless abandon and spent great energy protecting our most valuable asset: our selves. We tallied points and tempered and tantrumed as if neither of us had ever been adults. What we didn't know then was that we were not entering a competition where one wins and one loses. In the fighting, though, came clarity of goals: He wanted to be accepted, and I wanted to be heard.

Listening, in fact, took on superpower status for me because I had come to associate self-value with how much a person listened—or didn't listen—to me. Locked inside my thinking was the little-girl idea that if he did not listen to me, ask me questions, or look at me while I was talking, he was not very interested in who I was. I had never been good at offering glimpses of my soul to those who hadn't first earned the right by listening. And so my fear of never being known grew larger, into a demanding idol I worshiped every time I entered a discussion.

On the other hand, he told me Australians rarely offer questions; instead, they "one up" each other to avoid confronting their own pains. To help me further understand, he explained how the national psyche down under tended to be one of insecurity and sarcasm, methods cultivated for surviving an imposing U.S. culture that overshadows any sense of their own cultural pride or loyalty. Identity, he said, was a troubling issue for most Australians.

A lot of good my degree in cross-cultural communication did me now.

Still, I could not easily ignore the passions this man possessed and the convictions he carried. Albeit subconsciously, I decided I would do what I had done as a child when my family went fishing: I would wait until he seemed sufficiently tested, and then I'd return from the river, a better woman for the waiting but still empty-handed. Ready to grill something else for dinner.

By June we were back to riding bicycles around Central Park. On one particular Saturday, we started out politely enough. Then a "culturally sarcastic" comment slipped from his tongue. That did it. On what was otherwise a beautiful summer day in the park, and for the entire 6.2 miles around, we belted each other hard with emotion-packed sentences and hefty accusations. First me, then him in defense, then back to me, and around we went. I was exhausted by the time we returned to the apartment building, and not from the bicycle ride. This relationship business was taking its toll.

But for some reason—gluttons for punishment, maybe?—we went ahead with an already scheduled "special date" later that night. All the way to the subway, I argued with him about whatever entered my unredeemed mind, and I came close to turning around to go home. We stood outside the entrance of the subway, deliberating loudly, people passing barely noticing us, in typical New York fashion. Finally he convinced me that we should go anyway. We were already out for the night, he said, and we could still try to have fun. I was not so sure, but I was willing to believe him.

We ended up at a quaint Italian restaurant that sits in the shadow of the Brooklyn Bridge. Over wine and seafood pasta, we attempted to be nice, which was easier at this point for the Aussie than for me. After our dinner, he suggested we stroll across the bridge to enjoy the city lights and the river view. I agreed—there was little fight left in me by then.

Halfway across the bridge, we stopped to admire the New York skyline. I leaned against the railing as my eyes jumped from the Empire State Building and the World Trade Center to the South Street Seaport and the other high-rises. The lights glistened on the East River below us, and though I was still tired and smarting from the day's exchange, I felt certain that friends would have called this a "romantic moment."

Maybe he would ask me how I was feeling or if the evening air was too cool for me. Maybe he would invite me over to where he was standing to point out a view I had missed. Maybe he'd challenge me to a contest of who could throw pennies or stones the farthest into the river. Maybe he'd even take me into his arms for a little moonlight dance and let me hang around his neck so I wouldn't feel afraid.

Instead, I suddenly realized Mystery had come along on our date too. For this man from the Southern Hemisphere pushed out his forearm, grabbed my hand, and caught me completely off guard.

"You don't have to answer me tonight, but I want to ask you to marry me."

I almost fell sideways into the river as terror shattered my heart. I studied this man's face—his clear blue eyes, his trimmed brown beard, his slight smile—hoping he had had too much wine or had suddenly gotten a sense of humor. He hadn't. In fact, he was more serious than I had ever seen him.

I pulled back my hand, tightening my neck and shoulders, and asked, "Didn't you hear a word I said today? We just had a whale of a fight, and now you're asking me to marry you?"

He nodded. I froze. He leaned over and kissed me softly. I shook my head, astonished, and looked away toward the lights. Then he reassured me again that I did not have to answer him tonight. I didn't.

We rode the subway in silence. The next week in my living room, I told him I could not even think about marriage for at least a few months. I was finishing an emotionally draining writing project on racial relations, and I already felt pulled into unfamiliar territory. Perhaps the distance would be good for us, I reasoned. I was not saying no, but could we talk about this again in August? I asked. His head bobbed up and down in reluctant agreement although his shoulders shook a bit. Slowly, the man climbed out of the couch and slowly, cautiously, he stepped far away from me and walked toward his apartment.

That was a long and humid summer.

A symbol is something that is itself and yet also represents something else, like an idea. For example, a lake may be a lake, but it is also a feminine symbol, home to magical monsters or mystical powers. There are two general types of symbols: universal symbols that embody universally recognizable meanings wherever used, such as light to symbolize knowledge or water to represent life, birth, or refreshment; and invested symbols that are given symbolic meaning by the way an author uses them in a literary work, as the glass becomes a symbol of human frailty in *The Glass Menagerie*.

Far from the days of swim club and family camping trips stands a friend I have come to cherish: hindsight. I have looked at the world a bit since those early years and have observed a piercing contrast to the life I knew as a child. I have lived in neighborhoods as an adult where parents struggle simply to buy new shoes for their children, let alone ever consider a vacation for them. Reports from the evening news show me families in war-torn countries fighting just to survive the terrifying evil in their lands, while others rebuild crops and homes devastated from hurricanes or earthquakes— horrors kept far from my adolescence. All the while I sit here trying to understand why listening to my life is important enough to put on paper. In a book, for pete's sake.

I am hard pressed to justify it, and yet I am hard pressed *not* to. Perhaps communication is more than a luxury, more than a subject to be studied in college. Wrapped up in all that is human is a heart that must belong, wherever in the world it's been placed, and then connect to other hearts through the symbols of words. I've come to realize, though, that for a million different reasons, fear can steal those words and block the bridge to another's soul.

But I have also watched—and experienced—the hope that rises when someone is pursued for who she is. Is known as she is. And is loved in what she is. Language helps the healing; listening soothes the soul.

How grateful I am now for fishing poles, Coleman stoves, terry-cloth towels, and of course, the human care that each represents. Certainly my parents did not have to put their middle-class income toward giving my brothers and me so many unique experiences in the mountains or in suburbia. But they did, and though we might not have shared as many sentences or feelings as we did burgers or shrimp dinners, I see now that it was no accident God loaned us to each other during this time on earth.

Especially when we went camping at the lakes. *A lake may be a lake, but it is also a feminine symbol, home to magical monsters or mystical powers.* Nature's swimming pools. Lakes were also Christ's reluctant showcase for evening strolls to catch up with his friends. Those waters hold as many different memories as they do names: Lake Wobegon, Lake Champlain, Dillon Lake, Lake Erie. Each is a reservoir of symbols. It's funny how you can look at a lake for the first time and watch the past walking into your present.

And so the dirt road seemed familiar even though I had never driven down it before the summer of my thirty-eighth year. The New Jersey woods looked like a few other woods I had visited, though nothing in my memory confirmed I had been here. Three-letter word games, sleeping bags, and coolers filled the car as I drove with friends for a retreat at a state park and lake the June after I snorkeled in Jamaica. We had made the couple hours' drive west of New York to explore together the topic of how to live out our faith in our respective vocations. We were here to listen to our lives.

I helped one friend put up a small two-person tent and then joined others to hike down a wide trail. The smell of fresh woods and wildflowers floated in the air as sunlight jumped across bright green and yellow leaves. As we walked, dust kicking from our heels, questions popped out like branches from the trees. We heard portions of each other's stories and hopes for the coming week. Many had arrived tired, ready for some renewed connection with like-minded friends. Others were determined to find answers to hard questions they had encountered on their journeys. A few, like me, just wanted to see the lake.

Our conversation stopped when our trail was cut off suddenly at the edge of a huge body of water, smooth as glass. An enormous silence surrounded us as we each looked across the lake. No one moved. Faces calmed. Senses reveled. Tensions faded.

A few of us eyed a canoe near the water, and my stomach jumped with anticipation. I could barely remember the last time I was by a mountain lake, let alone on top of one in a canoe. Childhood images of camping fears and river loneliness were mysteriously challenged in my mind by an older assurance that Christian faith had provided. I think I even heard Someone whisper in my ear, "Never will I leave you, never will I forsake you." So I climbed inside the canoe with the others and began to paddle, smiling at the possibility.

In the center of the lake, we dropped our oars inside the canoe and allowed the breeze to take us where it would. We waited, closed our eyes, and let the sun warm our arms and faces. Within minutes, though, our attention was grabbed by a sudden movement beneath the lake's surface. A long current pushed the water into two narrow lines only feet from us, and my eyes grew huge from the idea of some creature stirring so close by. It had been such a serene moment; were we now about to see some prehistoric monster that hid in this lake? My heart went wild in the pounding.

Then I saw its tail. It was about as long as my forearm, wide and flat like the leaves we had passed on the trail. My mouth went dry, and my eyes did not blink. No one breathed.

Fear erupted into laughter when we discovered the reality below us. With smooth and graceful determination, a tiny smiling beaver swam around us, under us, and then beyond us, as if to challenge us to follow. I filled my lungs with fresh mountain air. We picked up our oars and paddled gently behind the beaver. Within minutes we approached the little guy's home, a colony of fallen trees and broken branches that had amazingly been built by a family of beavers.

Sometimes, if we are really lucky, wonder never leaves the child.

We stared a long time at the home. Then we paddled a distance from the home so as not to disrupt the animal's family time, marveling at the discovery. Back in the center of the glassy lake, we dropped the oars again, allowed the sun to warm us, and then with absolutely no warning and no time for my heart to argue, uninhibited delight flung my body overboard into the icy, beaver-filled water. For a woman my size, I made a remarkable splash.

And I swam.

I kicked my legs and pointed my toes heavenward. I flung back my head and watched white clouds crawl across blue sky. Arm over arm, I backstroked all around that tiny canoe in that New Jersey lake. And I thought about swimming, camping, and family homes, grateful to have known each. Then another friend jumped in to join me, and we laughed and swam until our bodies were numb and the skin on our fingers gathered like prunes.

After about a half-hour, we climbed back into the canoe, exhilarated by our temporary flirtation with prehistoric creatures, dripping from the adventure and full from the moment. We paddled back to the trail, plopped the canoe on the bank, and hiked up to our tents, still dripping, still laughing, still full.

I'm not sure how many life questions were answered that week, but I went canoeing and swimming every day. It was the best part of that summer.

The Glass Menagerie is one of American literature's greatest tragedies for one simple reason: Laura and the other characters confront the possibility of change and healing and choose instead to stay broken. Like glass.

Shortly after my fortieth birthday, I finished the book project on race relations, exhausted from the spiritual challenge it had presented, yet hopeful the book would do some good. Except for a few pages left to edit, the last chapter was written, deadline met.

I walked upstairs to the top-floor apartment and knocked on the door. Now I could direct what was left of my emotions to the unfinished business of the relationship with this man.

The Australian opened the door. His hair was cut short from the summer, and I realized it had been a few months since I had stood close enough to see his blue-gray eyes. Always the gentleman, he invited me in, offered me a cup of coffee, and pointed to a chair in the living room. I accepted all three and attempted small talk for a few minutes, something I had never quite mastered in my now forty years of life. That done, I jumped in.

"Your birthday is coming up. Are you interested in trying this dating thing again?" I asked with great sensitivity. The Aussie almost spit out his coffee. Then he studied my face to know if he should position himself for protection. He must have seen some semblance of sincerity (albeit tactlessness) because he agreed to think about it, told me what he had been doing during the summer months, and refilled my coffee. Caution was in the air, but only a slight breeze.

The season was changing.

By the end of the next month, I took him to a swanky seafood restaurant in SoHo to celebrate his birthday over fresh oysters and Australian wine. We did a moonlight ride on the Staten Island ferry and felt New York's harbor spray the deck, bringing a refreshing chill to the fall air. With the lights of the New York skyline before us, the water below us, and the company of each other, there seemed little necessity for words, a rare exchange of silence for two usually language-hungry souls. Faces calmed. Senses reveled. Tensions faded.

Days before, I had taken a long, hard look down the road of my future and concluded I did not want to walk there without the presence of this man beside me. In spite of all our arguments and resurrected emotions, in spite of all the delicate wounds that still needed attention, I could not argue with reality's gift of change and healing this man had brought to me. Perhaps the one thing I had always assumed was for other people—marriage, intimacy, connection—really was for me too. I knew I didn't want to leave the river that night empty-handed.

We had walked off the ferry and into the subway when, with absolutely no warning and no time for my heart to argue, I suggested we get married. This time, neither of us knew Mystery had come along on this date, and the eyes of the birthday boy sitting next to me grew big. He did not blink for a few moments, and both of us held our breath.

"So this is what it feels like, being asked?" he whispered. Finally he smiled, I did too, and I think we went back to our apartments engaged.

By Thanksgiving we told our families, and by January we held the small ceremony in the living room of our new apartment. After we exchanged life vows to listen to and accept one another, after we put rings on each other's fingers as symbols of our commitment, and after the pastor and his wife prayed that God would have mercy on us, we sang a hymn whose melody was based on Beethoven's Ninth Symphony, with full but still fragile souls:

Joyful, joyful, we adore Thee,
God of glory, Lord of love;
Hearts unfold like flow'rs before Thee,
op'ning to the sun above.
Melt the clouds of sin and sadness,
drive the dark of doubt away;
Giver of immortal gladness,
fill us with the light of day!

All Thy works with joy surround Thee,
Earth and heav'n reflect Thy rays,
Stars and angels sing around Thee,
center of unbroken praise.
Field and forest, vale and mountain,
flow'ry meadow, flashing sea,
Chanting bird and flowing fountain
call us to rejoice in Thee.

Thou art giving and forgiving,
ever blessing, ever blest,
Wellspring of the joy of living,
ocean-depth of happy rest!
Thou our Father, Christ our Brother—
all who live in love are Thine;
Teach us how to love each other,
lift us to the joy divine.

those people

(and the friends I almost missed)

> The beautiful is as useful as the useful, perhaps more so.
>
> —VICTOR HUGO

$f$ew things move me as much as an acoustic guitar playing a jazz solo. Whenever skilled fingers move up and down the frets, jumping across solitary notes on individual strings, my soul is immediately seized, my shoulders loosened. I close my eyes at the soothing sound. I relax. It is altogether different from the unified sound of a chord when a pick slides across all six strings at the same time to create a tone that supports the melody. That is nice too, but it is not the same. No, a solitary acoustic jazz piece from a guitar always guides my soul and makes me think of stones skipping across moonlit water: beautifully unique, peaceful, transcendent.

The songs of humans don't seem as easily recognized. Most of our lives, it as though we try to blend in with other notes, all the while hoping to find some distinction to define us, some solo to come into. We wait sometimes patiently, other times not, for anything, anyone, to tell us who we are and where we came from. Some of us crave an identity that will define and direct us, while others hurry past it, too afraid its demands will clog our lives.

Now from many miles and melodies away, I find myself asking how young, blond, suburban children in the 1960s and '70s ever knew who they were. Our worlds were full of people who sang and dressed and smelled like we did, who considered safety and comfort staples for life, songs that required only a few chords strummed in predictable rhythms. How then did we—how did I—muster the courage to venture far enough from home to discover even a whisper of…moonlight?

Maybe it began for me on my eighth birthday, when I watched some older Hawaiian women dancing the hula. Their brown skin swayed like the tropical breeze, their thick black hair adorned with orange and pink flowers bounced back and forth, their bellies wiggled to the beat of a brown-skinned man singing "Tiny Bubbles." My blue eyes could not look away from the dark, dancing women before me—I had never seen anyone who looked so opposite from me, and therefore I could not go near them. I was terrified, confused, and glad all at the same time.

The paradox of difference had entered my life.

"By that time Pooh thought of another song:
It's a very funny thought, if Bears were Bees,
They'd build their nests at the bottom of trees.
And that being so (if Bees were Bears),
We shouldn't have to climb up all these stairs."

— A. A. MILNE, *Winnie-the-Pooh*

The summer after the hula show was unusually hot, so my parents packed my brothers and me into the station wagon again. We were going for a weekend to cool off in a little town in Colorado's mountains only a few hundred miles from our house, but to me, a nine-year-old, we might as well have been driving to the moon. Even a trip across town seemed far away and, therefore, frighteningly unfamiliar to me. The interstate was not yet built in those days, and my dad had to take a two-lane mountain road: narrow, curvy, high. Close to the edge. Across twelve-thousand-foot peaks. Windows down. My brothers squealed at the adventure, my mother tightened her seat belt, and I held my stomach, hoping the peanut butter sandwich would stay there.

My dad told us the town where we were going had a natural spring that bubbled up out of the mountain and into a swimming pool the size of a football field. Somehow they had channeled the spring water into this massive cement hole and kept it open all year long for families like mine. Even in the icy winter. I didn't quite understand why we had to drive so far just to go swimming in a pool with bubbling water, but my dad said it would be a fun and new experience. I looked at him suspiciously. Around each corner and past each peak, my stomach turned a little more from both the winding road and the thought of swimming in a huge mountain pool with strange water.

Six hours later we pulled into the parking lot, and the sun pierced our skin as we got out of the station wagon. The air seemed the same as what we had left back in our neighborhood—hot and dry—so I still wasn't quite sure why we were here. Wasn't the mountain air supposed to cool us off? Maybe the water would provide what the hot summer sun could not: reprieve.

After my father traded a twenty-dollar bill with a skinny teenage boy for five pool passes, my mom grabbed my hand and led me to the women's changing room while my dad took my brothers to the men's. White plastic curtains separated women from toilets, but the showers knew no such privacy. In a large high room with dozens of showerheads, pale naked women marched under the steam, chatting with each other as if they were at a family picnic. Mothers scrubbed children and rinsed swimming suits. I pulled mine up over my nervous belly and waited for my mom to come from behind one of the white plastic curtains.

We walked into the sunlight and toward the cement spot my brothers had found for us. Mountains all around us, people packed across the massive pool, my head became hot and dizzy again. Then I smelled it: a horrible odor of rotten eggs and sour milk combined. Coming from the bubbling water. In the pool! I stopped walking, frozen in the stench. I groaned real loud and pinched my nose in protest. I refused to take another step forward and stomped my foot till it tingled.

No one noticed.

Within minutes my brothers had jumped into the deep end, my mother was wading in the shallow end, and my father was heading toward the diving board. I let go of my nose, scurried toward the metal ladder at the side of the pool and waited, tiny beads of perspiration sliding down my forehead. I watched my brothers laughing, my dad diving, and my mom standing. In the stinky, bubbling, strange water.

So I did what any nine-year-old who wants to be a part of her family would do: I jumped in. Reluctant but wanting to belong, I feared isolation more than this strange smelly water before me. Eyes shut hard, arms out like wings, I flung my body through the air and leaped into the pool.

It was not pretty.

When that water slapped my skin, I hollered so loud the nearby mountain probably shook, all the ladies in the showers probably jumped, and my parents probably turned bright red at the noise coming from their only daughter.

How did my dad forget to tell me that we were going to a natural *hot* springs pool?

I had jumped into the evening bath! Forget the wings, my arms flailed through the water looking for something to hold on to, my eyes exploded with sulfur stings, and my heart scurried faster than our old station wagon ever did on the highway. I paddled toward the edge like our dachshunds had done in the river, and I sprang up onto the dry cement. Shivering. Whining. Sobbing. I looked around at the crowds of faceless people, found my terry-cloth towel, and crawled down on my belly, still smarting. I glanced back toward the evil smelly pool, amazed and confounded that my brothers were still laughing, my mother still wading, and my father still diving.

Water in pools was not supposed to be hot nor was it to smell. In fact, it was supposed to be cool and clean. That's what I was used to and that's what I expected. This contrary encounter was both uncomfortable and jarring to my predictable little life, and I wasn't sure what to do about it.

This would be a longer trip than I had feared.

Crocodiles belong to the same group of reptiles, the archosaurs, that were ancestors of dinosaurs and birds. Azaleas are beautiful flowering, semi-evergreen shrubs or small trees that belong to the genus Rhododendron and the heath family, *Ericaceae*. Assets belong to their owner, regardless of who possesses them and regardless of whether they were purchased with borrowed money. Inhabitants from a particular region often speak with a single

major dialect belonging to that area. Priests who belong to
religious orders are sometimes called regular clergy because they
live according to a particular rule.
Belonging is part of the natural order.

I suspect my high school was like many others in a nation of suburbs in the 1970s: full of belongers who joined everything to avoid
the possibility—and therefore the pain—of not fitting in. We had
bulky guys who grunted a lot and belonged to the state champi-
onship football team; saucy girls who combed their sandy blond
hair hourly and belonged to the pep club; smart kids who belonged
to their studies and carried their thick heavy textbooks everywhere,
including the lunchroom and the bathroom; even dopers, as we
called them then, those teens with long greasy hair and bloodshot
eyes who could answer every question a teacher asked them if only
they could make it to class. They belonged to no one but each other.

Besides our immense longing to be a part of something bigger
than our insecure selves, another commonality connected each
clique at my high school, one none of us ever bothered to notice:
our pigmentation. Of course, we had various shades of whiteness
or hair color, some had more freckles than others, some brown eyes
instead of blue, but most of us came from European-American
middle-class families who parked their station wagons in the drive-
ways and went camping in the summers.

Uniformity was a way of life.

Across the years I have often wondered how the handful of kids labeled "different" might have felt among all this sameness, and I honestly do not know. Truth be told, I didn't even think about asking them then. When you are already a part of the status quo, the dominant group, it does not occur to you to wander far from that which is commonly understood. I suppose that which is unknown is too threatening or alarming, so why explore that territory if you do not have to? As a result, the most unexplored territory we'd ever entered was at parties and dances, where music and strobe lights bounced off our hearts and teased our hormones. Other than gender differences—and we were quite familiar with them—we knew little of contrast. We even avoided the local amusement park because some bulging football player told my friends and me that tough Hispanic girls from the city roamed the grounds looking for white girls to beat up. I believed him.

So when I became friends with a Japanese-American girl on the basketball team, I literally thought nothing of it. Yes, I noticed her quarter-moon eyes and charcoal black hair, but I liked the high-pitched sound of her laugh and her dry wit. She was a year older than me and worked harder than any other player on the team. Consequently, she was our starting senior guard in every game. Well respected. Quietly determined. Never missed a free throw or an opportunity for a good laugh. I, on the other hand, was lucky to be a substitute for even five minutes in each game, so for many reasons Janet had my easy admiration.

We enjoyed a mediocre season my junior year, the few victories and team spirit due mostly to Janet's gutsy efforts, humble leadership, and funny one-liners. (We probably would have been dead last had it not been for our starting guard.) When basketball games ended and spring began, my parents thought I needed something else to occupy my time after school. I began looking for a job, and my Japanese friend led me again.

"You can come work for my father," she said to me. Her dad owned a lawn-care business where he packed mowers, rakes, and hoes in the back of a truck and groomed the yards of some of suburbia's wealthiest residents. Janet joined her younger brother each spring and summer to work for her father. I liked the idea of being outside, so I agreed. My mother and father were glad, especially when they realized I would not be staying home to watch *Gilligan's Island* reruns on the black-and-white television in our basement.

For many afternoons and into the summer days, I joined this strong quiet family in trimming bushes, collecting mowed grass, and clipping hedges near sidewalks. Day after day in the hot dry sun, we worked, hardly exchanging a word, let alone a sentence, unless they were directions about caring for the next lawn. Sometimes Janet would simply nod as her father talked to her in a strange language, while I pretended not to notice how the unknown words clogged the air for me. Janet's father seemed older than he probably was; gray hair and lined face revealed both an unfamiliar tenacity and an uneasy mystery. Theirs was a serious interaction. No laughing. No resting. No playing. Janet was an obedient daughter, and this was business. Her family seemed determined to carve a successful place in American society, no matter how hard they had to work. As if they were afraid of losing something if they did not. So when I tried to initiate water fights or make conversation during working hours, my friend simply glared at me to stop.

I was confused. And tired. I was not used to such strenuous labor. So whenever I asked my friend why they kept the pace they did and where she got her sense of humor, since it obviously wasn't from her family, she simply looked away. Like some faraway secret locked the answer in her soul. Then Janet would just smile and tell me it was time to get back to work.

I only worked for Janet's father that one summer—it was all the physical labor I could handle. Janet never did help me understand what made her family so intense and so rigid in their quest to achieve. And I lost interest when my attention was easily diverted by softball tournaments and summer cookouts. Aside from working for the lawn-care service, life for me remained relatively easy.

But years later, after I had graduated from college, another Japanese friend explained to me what might have been the secret that drove Janet's family toward relentless security. With passion in her voice and hands waving through the air, her explanation to me went something like this: In the early 1940s just after the United States entered World War II—and around the time Janet's father would have been twenty-five years old—more than one hundred thousand people of Japanese descent were perceived as "enemy aliens" and placed in protective custody by the American government. Many families from Denver were sent to "holding camps" in

Wyoming, where they were forced into hard labor. Two out of every three of these Japanese "prisoners" were American citizens by birth; the other third were aliens forbidden by law to be citizens. But no charges were filed against these people nor any hearing held. The removal of families like Janet's was on ancestral grounds alone, simply because they were of Japanese heritage.

"Isn't it funny," my older friend concluded, face filled with intensity, "that even though World War II was the war that was supposed to eliminate such horrors, some of the same things were happening in your very own backyard?"

No, it did not seem funny at all to me. If anything, I suddenly felt confused and afraid but strangely glad for the job I had with Janet's family. I also felt ashamed—all at the same time.

"To become truly immortal, a work of art must escape all human limits: logic and common sense will only interfere. But once these barriers are broken, it will enter the realms of childhood visions and dreams."

—GIORGIO DE CHIRICO

The sun was dropping at the back of the clear blue horizon, sending bright orange and yellow streaks across the tropical sky. The colors matched the flowers that stood in the vases throughout our hotel room. My father had brought our family on our second Hawaiian visit just months before I graduated from high school—the year after my basketball season with Janet. Instead of the usual sweaters to warm us from the Colorado winter cold, we were in swimsuits and ocean humidity to celebrate the Christmas holiday. We had had a week's worth of the tourist trinkets and hula shows of Honolulu. For the rest of the Christmas break, my parents decided to bring us to Hawaii—the Big Island.

I guess they thought the holiday change would be nice. So instead of decorated evergreens, we were shaded by palm trees; instead of cranberries, we sucked on pineapples; and instead of ski slopes, we lunged across tennis courts. Though my brothers and parents were excited about the tropical adventure, I had grown to love the comfort of snowy December days with my high-school friends and did not look forward to the long plane ride away from them and *over* the ocean to this foreign island. No, I was not exactly sure why we had to come so far from home for Christmas.

Especially when I saw the beaches.

The morning after our sunset arrival, I walked out of our hotel room and onto the pool deck that hung over the beach. Before me were miles and miles of swirling blue waters, a few tiny boats bobbing up and down on top of the waves that crashed against each other. Gulls flew directionless above them. I could hear Hawaiian music vibrating from big black speakers that hung behind the pool's bamboo bar. My mother was on a lounge chair not far from the bar, reading a book, sipping some bright pink drink and stirring it with a miniature umbrella that pierced an orange slice and a cherry. My brothers were diving into the pool and talking to girls, and my father was on his way to a tennis match with the hotel pro. I sighed, wondering if it was snowing in Colorado.

Then I walked over to the fence that separated the pool area from the sea, looked over the edge, and almost fell sideways when I saw what was beneath us: The beach below was not at all like the soft, sandy brown stretch we had walked in Honolulu. This was hard stone, thick black rocks in a million different shapes that apparently had been formed from volcanic ash and now slapped any waves that tried to roll in and out. Their impenetrable form dared the waters—and any human being who was foolish enough to stroll across them. This charcoal black beach, with its piled castlelike rocks that sat beside rough waters, was not exactly inviting.

I leaned against the fence and turned my face toward the sun's warmth, closing my eyes and wondering how quickly this trip might be over. Maybe the sun would offer some reprieve from the broken Christmas tradition after all. Maybe somewhere on this island I would hear the story of the child born in the manger, smile at the new faith my high-school youth group had shown me it represented, and pray that our family would enjoy the time together—without too many arguments. Maybe I would get both a tan and a real conversation with my mom.

Then again, maybe...not. My mind jumped to Colorado

friends who were probably skiing together. And I wondered about the year ahead, one that meant graduating from high school and entering college, leaving the safe familiarity of the suburbs and exploring an entirely new world seventy miles away. I imagined how I would handle the changes. The sun felt good on my face because sometimes paths that lead toward foreign places invite a soul to hope.

And sometimes they provoke fear.

A shadow interrupted my revelry, and my eyes sprang open to the annoying presence of a twelve-year-old boy with blond hair, one whose parents had probably forced him to come here and left him by the pool unattended while they played golf. Suddenly he shot his head back into the sky and cackled a high-pitched sound that nearly shook the volcanic rock below us and made the umbrella in my mother's drink spin in circles. He folded his face in half, cackled again, and jumped up and down on his lounge chair as if it were a trampoline. Then he leaped from the chair to a plastic table where he all but tackled a silver can of soda, took a massive gulp, belched as loud as he had cackled, and without warning, heaved the can over the fence like he was playing left field on a Little League baseball team. Never mind the white bamboo trash bin a few feet from him. This brainless boy flung his soda can with all his might. Toward the lava rock. By the sea. And then the cackling juvenile jumped back on his chair. Up and down. He was clearly not a part of any social structure.

I was furious. Although I wasn't the least bit interested in exploring this strange beach, I did at least respect it enough to know that a silver soda can did not belong among its lava rocks. I glared at the stupid boy and made my way around the fence, down the path to the black rocky beach. The silver can was lodged between two huge rocks that sat about twenty-five yards from the path, close to the sea. I wiped my palms against my T-shirt, took a deep breath, whispered to God for help, and started out across the rock piles. Each rock was a different size, some with glassy-smooth surfaces, others with edges that stuck out like knuckles on an enormous black hand. Slowly, carefully, I jumped from rock to rock and made my way toward retrieving the unwelcome shiny object. I glared back up toward the ridiculous child, who by now was just as oblivious to his sin as he was to the gulls above him. I secretly hoped they'd drop him a reminder of their superiority.

Within seconds, though, my righteous indignation melted into absolute, paralyzing terror as I landed on one hard rock. I was by now about fifteen yards from shore, closer to the can than I was to the safety of the path, but I could not move an inch, forward or back. I had not noticed from the deck above one very important detail about this beach: It was loaded with black crabs the size of my hand, and they were crawling over every piece of hard lava. They skittered across the knuckled rocks like tarantulas, dozens and dozens of them, crawling, working, and searching for something to devour. Sweat dripped from my brow and onto my lips. The salty liquid tasted horrifying.

Fear prompted panic, and my arms chopped the air looking for something to hold on to. My eyes exploded with tear stings, and my heart pounded faster than any boat could ever travel. I sprang across the wave-beaten rocks and collapsed when I reached the path. But as I looked back at the crabs and the daunting sea behind them, I could not help but dart up toward the pool area. Shivering. Whining. Sobbing. I chewed on my sweaty upper lip, looked around at the crowds of faceless people, found my terry-cloth towel, and fell on a lounge chair beside my mother. Still shivering in the hot Hawaiian sun, I glanced back toward the dumb, evil boy and beyond him to the crab-infested volcanic beach where the silver soda can still sat incongruously. I turned away to see my mother still reading and sipping and my brothers still talking to girls. I was confounded by the fact that their lives always seemed so unaffected.

Why had we come to this strange place, anyway? Beaches were not supposed to be made of hard black rocks, let alone serve as home to millions of spiderlike crabs who dodged the waves as they slapped the rocks. And twelve-year-old blond boys were not supposed to violate nature's floor with soda cans. Besides, I was more familiar with beaches that were soft and clean, waters that were calm, and children that were considerate of the earth. That's what I was used to and that's what I expected. True, the sun felt good on my face here, but it did not provide enough consolation for my confused and jittery soul.

I thought a lot about cold, snowy Christmas mornings and didn't drink a single soda the entire trip.

"I am never afraid of what I know."

—ANNA SEWELL, *Black Beauty*

College life seemed an easy parallel to suburban existence. I naturally gravitated toward those who looked and acted like I did. My roommates, soccer teammates, fellow students, and church and Bible study group members: all were comprised of other young women and men who had come from outer urban areas or small towns and were going in the same direction. It was a comfortable and pleasant four and a half years, with few adventures and fewer internal travels.

But several years after my rocky and humid Christmas, a gnawing uneasiness invaded my private world and began to greet me each morning. At first it was just a soft "Hey!" that I'd quickly ignore as I'd walk out of my apartment and into the suburban classroom where I was teaching high-school English. Then it turned into a "Hey, what are you doing?" that got louder each time the alarm clock went off. Finally it started to scream, and I could no longer pretend I did not hear its demanding question: "Hey, what are you doing with your life? Why are you *here?*"

I was restless. Disillusioned. Tired of playing the same old six-string chords to the same old beats. Eager for some diverse sensations, some moonlight on the water.

So I left the high-school teaching position and enrolled at a religious graduate school in Virginia Beach. There this "need" for beauty, this creativity that had been asleep inside me for a long time, began to wake up. I devoured books, reference materials, journals, and lectures, spending more time in the library than I did making friends or visiting the surrounding sites. I read books on U.S. history, African-American literature, urban anthropology, creative writing, missionary strategies, cross-cultural communication, anything that introduced me to this world of...difference. Words, language, questions, insights, and stories fed me, moved me, changed me. And I could not get enough.

I returned to Colorado ready to let the food of my education nourish some sort of action. Across from the pond in Denver's City Park, I found an apartment in a one-hundred-year-old building with hardwood floors, big windows, and a cozy invitation to make a home. I did. Many evenings I enjoyed the quiet of solitary prayer and Bible readings, reflecting on both the truths of Scripture and the realities of city life beyond my window. I watched the Christ of the New Testament walking the streets of Jerusalem, interacting with the same people who walked by my apartment. I fell in love again with the compassion he offered the outcasts, the hope he gave the poor and the lonely, and I wondered what he might say today to those who did not feel they belonged anywhere in particular.

City life was seeping into my soul.

A friend told me about an after-school program for young children in a neighborhood a few miles from mine. I telephoned the woman in charge, offering to drive over each Wednesday to pick up some of these second- and third-graders and help out in whatever activity she had planned. So what if I was not from the same world or of the same hue? Or that I before had only worked with high-school or college students, never children? I had studied urban culture enough in graduate school to hold at bay any fears or misgivings I had of inner-city neighborhoods. I was academically prepared. And I had prayed. Yes, I gulped when one of my brothers told me about a few of his women friends who had been mugged "down there." But the "what are you doing with your life" voice rang loud in my heart, and now I feared the restlessness more than I did the unknown.

What I hadn't yet realized was that even good intentions can go awry when threatened by the unfamiliar. One minute you're pouring coffee for a neighbor, happy for the opportunity to give, glad for a moment to chat, when out of nowhere a stranger enters the room, interrupts your deed, and turns you cold and nervous—protective, even. Your coffee spills. Your emotions fly. You forget charity altogether.

Why? Because when we are really honest with ourselves, we know that virtue and violence, hate and help, disgust and decency, live side by side in the home of our hearts. For the soul that is trapped in the comfort of its own fear, outsiders call out that darker side.

I do not like admitting it. But that is how it is.

So when I first went to pick up a handful of children in one of

Denver's inner-city neighborhoods, my anxiety rose. I did not like the boarded-up buildings or the litter that lined the streets. Each time I stopped at a red light, I wanted to swing over and lock my car door if someone was walking by. My sweaty palms stuck to the steering wheel as I turned onto the street where the housing projects were. And when I pulled up beside the apartments where the children in the program lived, the saliva in my throat evaporated. My neck tightened, and I asked Jesus to save my soul. Again. Just in case.

There on the steps of the apartment stood a tall dark woman with long blue extensions hanging from her hair and covering half her face. She wore a Malcolm X T-shirt and short cutoff jeans. She was smoking a cigarette as she leaned against the door. The address number on the apartment above her matched the one I had been sent to, which meant I was going to have to encounter this woman if I was going to escort the children for the program. My heart jumped.

I turned off the ignition, opened the door, and took a deep breath. The blue-haired woman stared at me with a look that I was sure questioned my very existence, glaring at me the whole time I inched my way toward her apartment.

I cleared my throat and took careful calculated steps, stomach flipping, eyes opened wide. When I was within a few feet of her, I began to mumble something about the children's program, who I was (though I wasn't quite sure at that point), and whether she wanted her kids to come along with us. I stared at the ground for a few seconds, fumbled for the car keys in my pocket, and waited for her response. I glanced around, and when I saw only a blur of face-less people, my spine began to tremble.

What happened next was something I have never forgotten. With a clear, distinct, and lively sound, the Malcolm X woman laughed. She dropped her cigarette, smashed it with her shoe as if embarrassed she'd been smoking it, and looked into my eyes with a dignity I had not seen in many other people. Then her face stretched into a beautiful smile, and she extended her hand to me: "I'm Freda. Yeah, of course, my kids can go with you to the pro-gram. It's a Christian one, and it's good for them."

She didn't seem to notice how moist my hand was or how her smile had completely diffused my fear, slapping me back to reality. She simply opened the apartment door and let two small hand-some boys, who had been listening to our conversation, fall onto the porch. She laughed again, patted their heads, and told them to be good. The three of us turned toward the car, raced like we were in the fifty-yard dash, and flung open the doors. I flopped in the driver's seat, and we drove to the center.

I have since replayed our introduction a hundred times in my head. I have told my husband and friends about it and written on it in journals or articles. But until now I have never asked myself this most disturbing question: *Why in the world was I so terrified of Freda?* I did not even know this woman. What did I think she would do to me? Attack me with a knife? And where had I learned that? Why had I come to believe that low-income, urban black women were not supposed to be so friendly toward white suburban women? I suppose the media and high-school football players had tried to convince me that inner cities were places of violence and despair, where poverty turned people into criminals we should fear, making us forget how we all belonged to the same family of human beings. That's what I was used to and that's what I expected.

But that is not what I encountered.

That night the moon hid behind gray clouds, and I drove back to my cozy apartment shivering, whining, sobbing. To God. Not because Freda or her children had frightened me. But because of how I had reacted to them. No, I sobbed because I had come face to face with the evil inside my soul. I had encountered my own private biases and felt ashamed, confused, and afraid all at the same time.

Thankfully, though, the Christ of the New Testament talked a lot about forgiveness, and that was the word I heard him speak that night. I felt the strange and glorious joy that always comes when you offer him your sin. Like when you stand on the edge of moon-lit water and toss stones across the surface—the moment is beautifully unique, peaceful, transcendent.

"You may be shocked by these words coming from me. But on this pilgrimage, what I have seen, and experienced, has forced me to *re-arrange* much of my thought-patterns previously held,

and *to toss aside* some of my previous conclusions. This was not too difficult for me. Despite my firm convictions, I have been always a man who tries to face facts, and to accept the reality of life as new experience and new knowledge unfolds it. I have always kept an open mind, which is necessary to the flexibility that must go hand in hand with every form of intelligent search for truth."

—MALCOLM X, *Letter from Mecca*

I spent much of my twenties and early thirties avoiding any more waters that were troubling or strange. In fact, to this day I never have returned to the hot springs pool or the Big Island, though I suspect each might look different through older eyes. A mind's image of certain scenes tends to fluctuate through the years, making old familiar roads seem new again, as if you're strolling down them for the first time. Of course, sometimes the roads *are* new, and you are astonished at the wonder of discovery all over again. Flexibility can certainly be one of life's braver and therefore sweeter gifts.

But by the time I had turned thirty-four and left teaching to enter the writing world full time, I had grown suspicious of and indifferent to large bodies of water. They had teased me a few too many times in my youth, and I did not think I was interested in seeing if they would ever be friends again. Besides, I was sufficiently immersed in the urban community I now called home, sharing meals and math problems with families like Freda's who lived next door. Living *in* the city and commuting *to* the suburbs each day to teach at a small Christian college had provided more than enough incongruity for a while. Now I wanted nothing more than to stay in the city, develop my craft, and enjoy my new community.

So when my mother called from her home in Georgia and asked me to join her on a tour to Australia, I became hostile at the distraction it posed. Friends told me I was crazy not to jump at the opportunity it presented, but I was not so sure. How would I respond to three weeks of travel with my mother when I hadn't spent much time with her in recent years? How would it feel being so far from the familiar and traveling twenty hours over the ocean just to get to this huge island I knew little of? I hesitated, thanked her for the offer, and told my mom I'd get back to her.

There are times when little children must *rearrange* many of their thought patterns previously held, that is, they do if they want to grow, to become adults. Perhaps part of learning to belong, of discovering our identity, is unearthed in places where we least expect to find it.

Because I had nothing else on my calendar and she was offering to pay my way, I slowly realized that I could not say no. Maybe, I reasoned, this trip could serve a dual purpose: I could write an article on the world down under for some magazine and I could work on my relationship with my mom. Both seemed important opportunities I could not overlook. "You'll be the poorer for it if you don't go," pressed one friend. So exactly five years before meeting my husband, I visited his country. With my mother. For three weeks.

Working for one of those specialized travel agencies, my mother was an escort, responsible for the fifty or so retired people who had signed up for this Australian tour. I was the youngest in the bunch, discovering early on that chronological age really has little to do with an individual's vivacity and energy. While these seniors went bungee jumping over rivers or snorkeling over the Great Barrier Reef, I was nodding my head politely and reading tourist brochures. My mother, however, had other plans.

"Let's go for a ride in a glass-bottom boat. Out to the Reef. You'll like it," she said one day when her white-haired entourage had gone scuba diving or hiking. A glass-bottom boat? On the ocean? I had never even heard of such a thing, and the idea hardly seemed exciting to me. But before I could respond, she was buying our tickets and steering me onto the deck. I sighed. I stared at the vast horizon before me and felt a tinge of moisture gather in my palm. I prayed a silent prayer, asking God to protect us. Then in case he needed my help, I decided I had better study the safety features of the ship. At least on *this*, I would be sheltered, dry, and safely distant from any possibility of unexpected elements. At least there would be no jolting surprises, I told myself.

We sat across from one another in the back of the houselike boat on benches that formed a *U* around a large clear window in the floor. The salty breeze tickled our cheeks as the captain put the motor in gear and we left the harbor. Beneath my feet the dark blur of the sea swirled by, doing little to build my curiosity or confidence; above me hung a pale yellow canopy to shade us from the sun. I glanced back toward the harbor and wondered how the hiking was going for some of the seniors, wondered how the families were in my neighborhood back home. I looked toward my mother, who was happily engaged in a conversation with the woman next to her, tanned face stretched into a variety of smiles as she told the woman—and me—how she'd done this boat trip a hundred times and that there was no reason to worry. I fumbled with the straps on my life jacket and wiped the nervous sweat from my forehead.

After forty or so minutes, and with the harbor all but a tiny spot behind us, the captain cut the engine. He announced that we were about to see one of the most spectacular sites Mother Nature had ever given humankind. With great pride, he explained how no other place in the world was like this; no other island or country boasted such a distinctive reef, with coral so uniquely beautiful. It's magical, he told us. My mother nodded in agreement, her blue eyes trying hard to reassure me.

I wanted to believe her. But I was not used to waters that were beautiful—they had mostly been frightening, troubling, and therefore unapproachable before now. That is what I had come to expect in faraway lands of the unfamiliar.

But it is not what I encountered under the yellow canopy on the glass-bottomed boat.

Instead, my eyes were seized by the multilayered glory below us. Oranges, blues, and reds filled the ship's window floor: clear, alluring, alive. Sunlight reached around black rocks and castlelike coral; tiny fish swam by, chased by bigger, brighter schools of color. Green and brown reeds swayed like trees in the wind, and a surge of praise jumped from my heart to my lips at the majesty beneath me. Both the sight and the ocean calm hushed my soul and guided my spirit like stones skipping across moonlit water, peaceful, transcendent. I understood why they called this reef "Great."

After several moments of awe, I glanced up from the window to see how my mother was reacting. She, too, was smiling as she stared. But not at the ocean's depth—she was staring at *me*. All the time I'd been admiring the ocean's song, she had been watching me, enjoying the satisfying pleasure that comes from witnessing the face of human discovery. With all her heart, she was glad to share this moment with her daughter, to see me as I must have appeared years ago in childlike wonder. I smiled back.

We barely spoke a word that day on the glass-bottom boat, but that exchange connected us in a way language rarely had. We belonged.

For the first time in my life, the salty sea air tasted sweet on my tongue. I leaned back from behind the canopy, put my face toward the sun, shut my eyes, and listened to the ocean-quiet as it warmed my soul.

slow bones

(and the body I want to keep)

> Be properly scared and go on doing what you have to do.
>
> —FLANNERY O'CONNOR, in her last letter before
> her death from lupus, *The Habit of Being*

t he sand is soft beneath my feet, the morning sun warm on my shoulders, but the steps I take are not easy. Waves roll cold white water across my toes, and I watch the earth rearrange itself with each movement. My footprint presses the sand in different directions, jetting it out into tiny peninsulas where shells and driftwood look like miniature villages and lighthouses. If I am not careful, I will disrupt the villages and drag heavy legs across an otherwise serene and youthful beach.

It has taken most of my life to see that a beach is not something to be feared; if I pay attention, I will see it is full of life and certainty and vigor. From the crisp breeze and the white sea horses to the blue-green horizon and cottony clouds, a sandy shore invites a child to unending play, not uneasy caution, an adult to reflection, not unwarranted apprehension.

But my bones feel slow today, slower, in fact, than yesterday.

Yesterday, when I was younger, easy was a way of life. Smooth mountain air always called me outside for a tennis match in summer, a ski slope in winter, or a soccer game in spring. Because walking rarely interests a child, I ran or skipped year-round, youthful motion as natural as breathing. No matter where I was—whether on vacations with my family somewhere in North America or in a neighbor's backyard next door—I was invincible, my muscles strong, my coordination sure. Even when I hiked a steep mountain trail and stumbled straight down a hundred yards, scraping my teenage body against jagged rocks and sharp branches, I was not aware of my mortality. I simply brushed myself off, admired the red of the blood streaming from my knees, and climbed back up the mountain.

Maybe I did not want to be aware then. The young, I think, live in a perpetual state of carefree abandon, where risk is second nature and age translates to them in terms of gain, not loss. Simply put, decline is not in the vocabulary of youth.

How then did it slip into mine these days?

At this sandy place in my early forties, my joints do not work as once they did, and the ache of each step signals the direction I am headed. Walking has evolved from dull to demanding, and running or skipping has become almost impossible. Perhaps, like

Jacob, I wrestled too much with God in my twenties and thirties, since now the socket of my left hip is permanently wrenched. Modern doctors call it arthritis, describing it as a deterioration of the cartilage between bone and socket that limits your movement, usually affecting people in their sixties or seventies. I know it as a recurring dagger that pierces my hip when I put one foot in front of the other or try to pretend I am sixteen again. Some days are better than others, of course, depending on the weather or the state of my soul or the activity of my lifestyle. Regardless, it is a result, the specialists say, of both genetics and traumatic impacts that might have occurred from falls down mountain trails or collisions in athletic events. Whatever the reason, they told me (when I was only thirty-five) that it is just a matter of time before they should replace it with a "medically advanced" plastic hip. Probably within five years. As if I am replacing a car when it has turned over 200,000 miles. Make it good as new. Make me young again.

I am not ready to be old.

Nor am I ready to lose a body part I've had for more than forty years and replace it with a new and improved one, for heaven's sake. Truth be told, the very idea of such surgery fills my eyes with liquid fear and upsets my stomach with rancid dread. So I push it away a bit and stare back toward the morning waves as they pour their vigor onto the sand beneath my feet. And I slow my steps to adjust accordingly because that seems to hold reality at bay a little longer.

"Our mortal lives hurtle toward extinction, that vast 'Times up!' surprise of the moment everything stops, and something timeless and uncontrollable begins. In-between we rush, blather, numb, avoid, consume; we kill time with a chainsaw, burn it like trash, anything to club down the fear there is no meaning."

—FREDERICA MATHEWES-GREEN, *At the Corner of East and Now*

Nothing ever really prepares you for a funeral. No matter how much you've admired the determination of an aging relative or how many distractions—and regrets—have kept you from spending time with her, the dark fact of death's intrusion always feels unexpected and unwelcome. It is a brush against your own frailty.

Almost five years ago I attended the funeral I never thought would arrive. Only a year before I had visited my old college town where my grandma lived, the place where now I joined my family in the Colorado morning sun, still and serious like the gravestones around us. An uneasiness I barely remembered welled up in me, catching me by surprise. Cousins, aunts, and familiar but unnamed faces climbed from black cars and greeted one another with stares and wordless nods. My father and his brothers circled around a gray marble marker, cleared their throats, and turned coins in their pants' pockets. I fumbled in my purse for a tissue—just in case—and joined the silent waiting. Wasn't I supposed to be sad?

As we stood in the cemetery, I felt a familiar tension settle over us like the hot summer air. It was the kind I had felt as a young girl at so many family gatherings, the same tension that somehow calls people who hardly know each other, "family." Only last year I had been with these people, with my relatives in this town; we had eaten birthday cake with pink frosting flowers on it and admired black-and-white photographs of our family in a thick black album: Uncle Jim as a baby, Aunt Joan as a girl on the farm, my grandfather as a teenage baseball player.

Though we shared a heritage and a last name, we talked with one another at the birthday celebration as if we were meeting each other for the first time, introducing ourselves with labels and details usually reserved for formal dinner parties or conference meetings. But it hardly mattered how we interacted with each other: we had come to honor the birth of our Czech matriarch. Grandma was turning one hundred years old. We marveled at the feat and rejoiced at the example. We joked about who else might win such a prize, and we sang in hope that this woman's life—and ours, too, for that matter—would go on forever. I never realized before just how unifying the happy birthday song can be.

It's funny how family has a way of freezing time, keeping feelings and emotions and perceptions from changing over the years. Even thirty-eight-year-old women can become little girls again in the presence of distant relatives.

Now, though, less than a year later, we were gathering on this June morning not for life and birthday cake and photographs but because of death. Not more than six months after her one hundredth birthday party, my father's mother died in her sleep. Natural causes, the doctor confirmed. She'd given in, as she used to tell us she would one day.

"What good am I doing at *this* age after all?" she'd ask anyone who was willing to listen. But before we would answer, she'd announce, "Ah, I'm pert-near good for nothin'!"

No matter what she may have felt in her final years, there was no denying that my grandma had lived a full life, the small-town pastor now reminded us as he stepped into the center of the circle to begin her memorial service. God had granted my grandmother many gifts in her one hundred years of living; she in turn had used them well, touching many people along the way. The dark-haired clergyman spoke to us with certainty. She had taught painting and ceramics at the senior center, played bridge with her friends each week until she outlived them all, and sent birthday cards to or knitted afghans for each of her twenty-five grandchildren until her hands could no longer move like they once did. A few years back, her busy life and numerous community activities had even earned her the town's senior citizen of the year award. Yes, God had allowed Grandma to live a long and full life.

I knew this was true, and the pastor's eulogy brought some reprieve from both the awkwardness of the gathering and the Colorado sun. Though I didn't remember much talk of God back then, I did remember Sunday nights at Grandma's house. We'd watch Tinkerbell paint the television screen for the Walt Disney show, drink Pepsi-Cola in clear glass bottles, and savor a traditional Czech dinner: dill gravy, dumplings, pork roast, and jelly kolatches, my grandma's specialty. I remembered backyards with clotheslines and barking dogs, cow smells from neighboring farms at family reunions, softball games with my cousins and uncles in makeshift fields.

I looked over the somber faces of these same cousins, uncles, and aunts now gathered around my grandmother's casket and shifted my weight from side to side. A portion of my past was shared with these people, and yet we hardly knew each other. I took a step back as I glanced again across their faces. Some stared at the grass beneath them, others wrestled with teary emotions. It seemed the closer we came to aging, the less we came together.

My memory jumped again, this time to when I was a nineteen-year-old college student, living only a few miles from my grandma and trying to visit her between soccer games, classwork, and social events. Each time I came, she would cook a special meal for me, tell me stories about Grandpa Joe or about raising their seven children on the farm during the Great Depression. Then she'd remind me that keeping busy was her secret to living a long life, though she wasn't really sure why she wanted one. She didn't believe much in anything any more, she'd tell me, except family and moving her bones, wondering some days why she should bother with either, wondering what was next for her. Each time she talked, I would nod attentively while my mind raced to college life and friends and soccer tournaments. And so I missed the sorrow of her words; instead, I'd smile politely at my blue-eyed elder, still lost in my own life, and would promise to come by more often. But youth's gains distracted me, and visiting Grandma dropped to the bottom of my priority list.

By the time the preacher finished his eulogy and prayer, I felt the cloud of tension and regret weighing on my shoulders. I glanced again at the faces and trees around me and realized that the death of this busy matriarch was now forcing me to confront my own cluttered life. I trembled. And as admirable as Grandma's long life was, I wondered if her final years were spent avoiding the end, busying her life with classes and meetings and photo albums. And I wondered if my busy life wasn't just a younger version of hers. I meant no disrespect—I had come to appreciate her longevity and tenacity in a century marked by much tragedy and despair. Yes, I gloated at her accomplishment. Still, I knew how much Grandma—how much I—feared the reality of decline, the fact that the body would not keep up with the mind.

Self-sufficiency is a prized possession for second- and third-generation immigrant families who know what it means to forge a new life. It is not easily relinquished.

Grandma was never ready to be old. Or dependent. Or unable. Instead, like a hungry baby clings to her bottle, my grandmother clung to the idea of being young and active (the two always went together in our family) for as long as she could, as if that in itself would nourish her with meaning or significance. Maybe Grandma believed deep in her soul that there was nothing to look forward to beyond this earthly life, that sore bones and art classes and grand-children were all there were, the sum total of a hundred years. Goal met. Had she measured her life in numbers, counting years and children and grandchildren the way bankers do dividends? Did she expect us to do the same?

Suddenly old age seemed more of a burden than a reward, and I feared it.

As I looked up into the cloudless sky that June morning of her funeral and we walked back toward our cars, I cleared my throat. Then I wiped the moisture from my palms with my tissue. I real-ized Grandma had indeed shown us how to get old. But I think she had forgotten to teach us the part about *growing*. Because in this cemetery and among this family, I realized *getting old* and *growing old* are not the same thing.

A tiny wet tear ran down my cheek at the thought. I let it fall off my chin and onto the grass in the cemetery.

"The memory is a living thing—it too is in transit. But during its moment, all that is remembered joins, and lives—the old and the young, the past and the present, the living and the dead.... A sheltered life can be a daring life as well. For all serious daring starts from within."

—EUDORA WELTY, *One Writer's Beginnings*

The noon sun has inched toward the center of the sky, and this beach is uncomfortably hot. Even a slight gust of wind would be nice right now, but there is none on this humid, fiery day. The sand is burning my toes, and sticky moisture is gathering up and down my arms. In front of me, the cloudless blue of the sky blends into the sea. I squint, and in the distance I see a tiny spot of a sailboat. Its sail is loose and straight, not curved or full of air like you see in the postcards. The boat seems stuck, tossed slowly by the waves around it. It does not move with any speed or finesse, and I wonder how it will make its way back into the harbor. It is hard to go anywhere in such still air, such heat.

When there is no wind, there is no motion.

I limp slowly toward the water, hoping it will cool my skin and soothe my achy legs. An orange-and-blue beachball suddenly bumps me on the back and soars out into the waves. A sandy child not taller than my hip and wearing a sailor's hat chases it just inches from me, splashing drops of ocean across my arms in the process. I gasp at the shock from the cold water.

My body once knew the same agility as the child. Not long ago, I was kicking white-and-black leather balls across freshly mowed grass at soccer tournaments in the town where my grandma lived. The fall air on my face, the challenge of constant motion between sprints and jogs that soccer requires, the joy of teamwork and strategies, and the total exhaustion that came from ninety minutes of nonstop play—each brought forth from me an extraordinary amount of youthful energy. Then, well into my thirties, I played soccer on coed recreational teams, in pickup games at parks, or with indoor women's leagues. I made short wall passes with midfielders, took direct kicks twenty-five yards from the goal, and sent the ball in the air from a corner kick during offensive attacks. I sprinted and turned and ran the length of the 110-yard field, my legs cooperating with my passion, my body keeping up with my mind. Rarely did I twist an ankle or pull a muscle in my twenty years of playing for different teams. And it didn't matter where or when I played or if we won or lost; the sport itself was enough to keep my busy soul feasting, my ego young. In fact, I always thought I would be kicking and passing and shooting on goals until I was at least one hundred years old or until I could walk no longer. Whichever came first.

Obviously, I am not one hundred today. And after too many kicks in too many games, I found running became a little too difficult. At first I assumed a year off would be enough. But the aching in my hip joint after merely jogging through my neighborhood suggested otherwise. Arthritis had set in. No matter. Someday, I'd tell myself, gritting my teeth, someday I'd put on my cleats again and head back onto the field.

Those *somedays,* I now realize, are windless moments in sailboats in which you keep hoping for some sort of change in the weather, even though the forecast never even calls for a slight breeze.

The tiny child with the sailor hat dives on his ball and falls into a wave. The blue-and-orange plastic sphere is carried away and he chases it, splashing me again in the process. I jerk back. Behind him a short, plump mama follows him, laughing nervously as she looks at me. She chases the ball with him. She helps him keep his hat on, a protection from the sun's rays. My ankles are covered with moving water, and I douse some salty sea across my arms to fight the noonday heat. I walk (at shin level) in the water for a long time, watching mothers and sons chase beachballs on the beach, and I wait for the tide to go out.

These days I am realizing that a body's movement is never guaranteed. Anything could happen suddenly to end my days of walking or moving or even turning my head: a fall down some stairs, an accident in the car, a collision on a bike. Anything. And the thought of such loss grips more fear from me today than the sea itself.

"Aw, youth is wasted on all the wrong people!"

—NEIGHBOR, in Frank Capra's film *It's a Wonderful Life*

In the second semester of graduate school, I enrolled in a writing course taught by a former editor of the *New York Times*. I was a tired, twenty-eight-year-old, high-school English teacher and soccer coach, far from Colorado, ready to apply the discipline I learned in the athletic world to an area I'd only winked at before and from a distance: academia. I'd never taken my education as seriously as I wished; perhaps it was the arrogance of youth or a lack of interest or sheer laziness (or all three), but I had hardly been the model student I hoped my own students would become. Consequently I wanted to prove to myself that I could master the books in this Virginia graduate program while still maintaining some sense of personal sanity. Life was reduced to studying, daily jogs in the park, reading, practicing with a local women's soccer team, and writing papers. Nothing else. I could almost always be found at the library, researching for a paper or preparing for an exam. My only goal was, well, to discover my brain.

People and relationships were not part of the game plan.

The classroom buzzed that first day of writing class. This was a popular course on campus, so almost every seat was full and a line of students waited outside the door, hoping to be added to the class roster. I targeted an empty desk toward the back of the room, plopped my books on top of it, then sat and waited. I eavesdropped on a few of the conversations around me: southern accents discussing last semester's grades or this semester's assignments, trading insights and phone numbers like children do secrets.

A white-haired man with thick glasses interrupted the chatter by clearing his throat and fumbling through some files until he found a wide green-and-white paper with black print on it. He read the alphabetical list of students' names in a dry raspy voice, looking up to study the face of each who responded "here" or "present" when his or her name was called. With a few, he asked knowing questions: how their parents were or if their studies were progressing well. His manner was friendly but commanding. He wore his newspaper years well.

By the time the professor had reached the *K*s and was trying to pronounce my last name, the door creaked open. I thought perhaps the hopeful students outside had grown impatient. Instead, a skinny, dark-haired man of about twenty-five entered. His mere presence demanded our attention. His face seemed young, though he struggled to keep it focused. The student's hands and arms curved like broken twigs, and he could not stop their shaking. In fact, he could not seem to control many muscles in his body; all he could do was push the tiny stick at the end of his armrest to steer his motorized wheelchair into the classroom.

He had cerebral palsy.

The young man moved slowly into the class and parked his chair about ten feet from the professor. I'm quite sure I was not the only one staring at him by this time, because a heavy quiet moved through the room. It was as if our looking stole any sound that might have come from the rest of us able-bodied individuals who had walked or rushed into the classroom. Using our legs. Directing our own steps. Moving easily.

After fumbling through more files, the professor glanced over at the man in the wheelchair, nodded his head, and simply continued reading aloud his roll call from the green paper. As if nothing extraordinary had just happened. As if a young man who could not walk or obviously use his hands even to sign his name had not just entered *this* class, a *writing* class.

"Kadlecek?" the white-haired professor queried, eyes searching across the twenty-five or so students before him.

I was still staring.

"Kadlecek?" This time, the sound of my name snapped me out of my gawking, and I almost jumped out of the seat. I cleared my throat and mumbled, "Yes. Um. Here, sir."

I got a glare from the editor-teacher as he studied my face. Then he continued calling out names. When he got to Williams, the wheelchair-bound student opened his mouth to respond. But no noise came out at first. His head moved from side to side while his eyes blinked open and closed. His right hand started jerking up and down. His tongue struggled hard to form some coherent language, and finally, with long pauses in between the words, he uttered, "Ye-e-es. I...am...Torey...Williams. Sorry...I...was... late, Pro...fess...or...The...traffic...was...bad...out...there."

The professor and most of the class burst into laughter at the student's comment. And then with the same intense labor he had mustered for his joke, Torey Williams's shaking face grew into a clear, full smile. Strong. Firm. Undaunted. Eyes opened, teeth shining, joy lingering.

I, however, did not laugh at Torey's joke. Was not able to. In fact, I was still staring, wondering how in the world he was going to make it through the semester. How would he write his papers? How would he hold his books or take notes during lectures? Who would help him type or study or tie his shoes, for that matter? How did he feel being completely and absolutely dependent on other individuals for simple daily tasks most of us took for granted? The mere question collapsed on my soul like an agonizing black night.

Self-sufficiency is not easily relinquished for third-generation immigrant families.

A tall bulky guy in front of me interrupted my nightmare with a thick stack of white papers and told me to pass them back. I obeyed. The professor explained each assignment on his syllabus, each expectation for the semester. We would write seven essays, read three books, review and discuss our individual work before the entire class. Each student would comment on and edit another's papers. Once the assignments were complete, we would write a final essay exam. In class.

I shot my eyes toward Torey, afraid for what these expectations meant for him. Talking was obviously not easy for him, yet the professor was requiring ongoing discussion during each class session. His hands couldn't hold a pen for more than a second, yet the professor was requiring we edit each other's work. And he would not be able to ask someone else to type his final exam like he probably would his papers, yet the professor was requiring an in-class essay be written at the conclusion of the course.

I suddenly cared very little about writing and a great deal about physical mobility. As I stared at Torey that day in class, my mind jumped again to the dark terror of what *I* would be like if the use of my legs suddenly were taken away. What sort of woman would I be if my hands unexpectedly grew crooked and bent or if I could not formulate sentences quickly and let them roll easily off my tongue? How would I manage to make it through each day if I could not watch one foot follow the other, if the muscles in my legs would not help me jog around the neighborhood? Or if the joints in my arms and legs and ankles stopped cooperating with the rest of my nerves and ligaments? What if my head shook so much I could not focus on the face of a friend or express my thoughts?

What if—God forbid—I could not take care of myself and my need suddenly became as exposed and public as an open wound?

Sometimes an active imagination is a horrifying intrusion. It can send you swirling into an excruciating pit, hundreds of feet from the comfort of reality and riddled along the way with hideous emotions that knock the wind from you. And when there is no wind, there is no motion.

During the next couple of months, I didn't learn much about the craft of writing in our writing class. I didn't listen well to the lectures of the professor or the comments of the other students. Maybe it was because the professor himself rarely came to class; he was fighting a life-threatening illness, one which he never expected during his first years of retirement after a long career in journalism. Maybe it was because my fellow students seemed more interested in people's comments on the content of their essays than on their style of writing.

Maybe, though, if I am really honest with myself today, I didn't hone my craft much that semester because I was busy watching Torey—terror-struck by his situation. I watched how difficult it was for him to interact with others; making friends or telling stories required great physical effort on his part. I watched him steer his chair and struggle simply to open a book. I watched how long it took for him to articulate words and sentences, and yet how quickly a smile could spread across his face. I'd glance from the professor or the chalkboard to the light in Torey during every class session, and though I didn't realize it at the time, the life (and dis-ease) of this young man forced me to confront my own.

How much I clung to the idea of being young and active, as if that in itself would nourish me with meaning or significance. Maybe I believed deep in my soul that bones and muscles and mobility really were the fuel for achievement, respect, and meaning. After all, hadn't Kadleceks always believed that personal independence and individual success were trophies to cherish, awards that were expected to ensure a long lifetime of satisfaction and fulfillment? If a person could not retain her physical mobility, what possible usefulness would she have? Wouldn't she be "pert-near good for nothin' "?

So without ever speaking a word to me, Torey asked me to take a long hard look at my legs and ankles and athletic abilities. Was I measuring my life in movements, counting regular jogs and soccer games and daily tasks as the sum total of my worth? Did my ability to maneuver my body up stairs and into classrooms or offices and around sidewalks or soccer fields reflect my value as a human?

Though I could not articulate it then, watching Torey made me deeply afraid. I see now that the advantages of health and youth were a burden I did not know how to bear.

Because, while independence plays a joke on those of us who are perpetually self-sufficient, dependence threatens our dignity. Torey seemed to know the secret of staying someplace between the two, remarkably aware of his beautiful individuality while living daily—and literally—at the mercy of others. I, on the other hand, earned a *B* in the writing class and unconsciously entered an internal debate between insecurity and assurance that would last longer than I ever want to admit.

"Is there a more fundamental fact of human existence? I was born in pain, squeezed out through torn and bloody tissues, and I offered up, as my first announcement of life, a wail. I will likely die in pain as well. Between those brackets of pain I live out my days, limping from the one toward the other."

—PHILIP YANCEY, *Reality and the Vision*

The breeze now has picked up and the afternoon sun has crawled across the sky, hiding every now and then behind gray-white clouds and softening its rays on top of my shoulders. Ocean waves sing a constant, peaceful rhythm, and their white foam forges new lines on the sand as I walk next to them. I hum a hymn—can't remember the words but the refrain says something of the deep, deep love of Jesus.

Beach air is fresh and full, and I breathe it in slowly, carefully, filling my lungs with its vigor. Though it's only a few hours from this place, the busyness of city life seems far away, and I am amazed again at how living in the city can heighten your appreciation for nature. Even the pain in my hip, the arthritis, is slight. The dagger has disappeared for a little while, and my legs feel unusually strong, enough to keep walking toward the reef a mile down the beach. Maybe it has been the rest in the sun. Maybe the coolness of the water on my legs when earlier I braved wading toward the waves, but I am not minding the stroll right now. Although my steps are slow, there is something right about the pace. I guess I notice more this way, hear more, taste more: the salt in the humidity, the laughter and shouts of the children, the young friends rubbing suntan lotion on each other's backs, the gray-haired couple wandering hand-in-hand along the sand. No one hurries here; no one carries much more than a book and a blanket. Busyness is a foreign land.

To pause at the shore of Mystery is to hold your fears up against its magnitude. Its enormity alone reminds a soul that she is small, so, so small. And that recognition is strangely soothing. It is to be part of a silence—a hope—that always floods the moment when you stand before such glory.

I watch the surfers as they float on their boards like shipwrecked passengers on rafts. It is a gentle afternoon, not much good for surfing. They do not seem to notice the small plane flying over them, imposing its engine noise on the quiet of the moment. I think of a friend who has jumped out of that same size plane more than twenty times. Intentionally. Skydiving. She loves the thrill of it, she tells me, and would do it twenty more times if she could afford the time and the expense. Never mind that a few of her friends have lost their lives because their parachutes did not open or something went wrong with the fall. Skydiving is invigorating and exciting, she says.

As if walks on the shore are not enough.

On this sandy beach in my forties, after a decade of trying to stop my body's decline, I am learning to be content with ocean breezes and colorful clouds—for they have provoked another type of awe and resignation in me altogether. They remind me that I cannot do what I once could, that the ground I walk on is always moving while the sky above me is always changing. So I watch the surfers and the planes and the changing sand and I confess: I feel better on days when my heart rate is calm, my palms are dry, and my boundaries are clear and defined. I suppose enduring any kind of degenerative disease makes your limits apparent and your respect for comfort greater.

On the other hand, I argue with myself, risk-taking is a good and natural part of life. It is. But now, as a middle-aged woman, I prefer my risking well done and surefire. Not raw or bloody or barely cooked. Yes, give me manageable, pain-free risk, please, the kind that stirs your soul without hurting your body.

I step on a seashell I do not see. Its sharp edge pokes into the sole of my foot and the thoughts in my head. I chuckle at the interruption and pick it up, turning the ocean ornament over in my hand. I see its orange spiral shape as a pointed caution that I cannot control what drops onto my path. I can, however, as my Christian conscience suggests, try to enjoy the gifts of the day, a day at the beach. The sand and shells, the breeze and sounds, all can be tools for feeling alive—at the very least. Funny, I don't think I would have noticed them ten years ago.

The tide moves stronger now, and I turn back toward the place where I started.

"Affliction is able to drown out every earthly voice...but the voice of eternity within a man it cannot drown."

—SÖREN KIERKEGAARD, *Christian Discourses*

At forty years old I was walking with the same hip God—not medical technology—had given me. I had wrestled with my weakening joint and its compensations for seven years, going back and forth between denial and horror, overactivity and lazy excuses. I tried desperately to find some comfortable place of acceptance. Still, a limp was defining my stroll more and more, and though they meant well, friends, colleagues, or family members worried whenever they walked somewhere with me. Would I be all right if we went up these stairs, they'd ask, or down those streets or around these corners? Could I handle the distance or cope with the challenge? Some would even take my arm like nieces do great-aunts as they walk together over icy sidewalks, then they would talk at me as if I had just stepped out of a nursing home.

As if I were the sum total of my limitation, my limp and my "handicap" the determining features of my identity and existence.

In response, I'd sometimes exaggerate a rhythmical dip to the ground, swing my cupped hand back and forth as I walked and say it was just part of living in the 'hood. We'd laugh and change the subject to politics or religion. Other times I would increase my pace and speed, challenging them to try to keep up, and reminding them—and myself—that, hey, I hadn't played competitive soccer for nothing. I was still an athlete after all. But sometimes, if I had searched my heart and paused with God, I would simply announce that I was developing a new understanding of my mortality, that I was no longer invincible like I had once believed, growing up in the Colorado Rockies. At those moments, I would take their arms for help.

Soon I understood that pride has a way of popping out of your heart like a jack-in-the-box. You're never quite sure when he's going to jump out and demand attention. Or if he'll return to his box licking his wounds and acknowledging defeat. So you do your best to keep him in his place and control the surprises. You get on with the business of living.

That's why I said yes to a few friends when we decided to ride bicycles around the Dingle Peninsula of Ireland's southwestern coast. Since it was the summer before my fortieth birthday, part of me was determined to see if I could hang on to some thread of agility. Besides, one doctor had told me that strengthening the muscles around the hip joint would delay surgery and reduce the pain, so I had begun bicycling as a substitute for jogging. Living in the city made it easy for me to ride the few miles to my office or a meeting with a friend as both a transportation alternative and a form of exercise. I enjoyed this new sport. Besides, bicycling seemed a fun way to see a new country and restore some physical confidence at the same time.

That is, until my friends told me we would average between twenty-five to thirty-five miles a day for seven straight days. Then I felt a little queasy. My palms got a little sweaty at the thought that maybe my legs—and my pride—would not last the distance or survive the daily trips for an entire week. And failure would have thrown salt on an already sore ego.

It did not help that just weeks before we left New York, a specialist suggested I have an MRI to see how, or if, the cartilage in my hip had deteriorated since the last time. MRI, they told me, was short for Magnetic Resonance Imaging: a staggering piece of medical technology where you lie perfectly still, strapped into a long cradlelike tube and pass under flashing lights at the slowest rate in the world. Loud clicking sounds all around you. For month-long minutes.

I cried the whole time. And this was just sophisticated picture-taking. Forget about the possibility of surgery.

With the clicking tube far behind me and no new outlook on my hip, we arrived in Ireland on a cool, rainy afternoon in August. After a long bus ride from the airport, we found our bed and breakfast and rested, hoping to recover from jet lag before our first ride the following day. The next morning we would meet our local guide, Cearran, who would give us our bicycles and maps. He would then take our suitcases to the next inn while we spent the day riding and exploring the Irish countryside. This was what the week's routine would be, and I was anxious about the demands of the schedule.

I don't know if it was the music of Cearran's Irish accent or the dance of the balmy sun across the countryside that calmed both my stomach and my heart rate that first morning. But as soon as I mounted my bicycle and saw the wonder of the island's green, my fear of defeat, of relinquishing my abilities even, stayed at a distance. That first day, at least.

And so we rode. Along coastal cliffs and sheepy hills, past stoic churches and castle ruins and ancient pubs, next to solitary farmhouses and mellow cows, and through small, quaint villages where people waved at us as if they'd known us all their lives. We parked our bikes outside pubs and talked with locals over Guinness and shepherd's pie. We laid the bicycles down on beaches so we could swim on the other side of the Atlantic. We set them against rocks or trees so we could explore the hills and remains of a history that was both bloody and gracious. And at night after rich ample dinners, I'd fall asleep bone-tired and immensely satisfied from the day's accomplishment. Even my fingernails were tired.

Until the next morning. When, still fingernail-tired, I'd sit with my coffee for a few stern moments and battle the possibilities of the days. Could my body keep going? Was I being too cautious? Had I reached my limit?

But each new morning, faith whispered and pointed me beyond the doubts to the Irish hills out the window. Nature's beauty is persuasive; my soul had to respond.

Because for me, everywhere I looked—and smelled and listened—on this peninsula was a writer's feast. Around each corner a new scene teetered on the point of poetry. And the day we laid our bikes at a bay's edge, the remains of a fifteen-hundred-year-old castle behind us on one side and a narrow winding road on the other, my muse all but jumped out of my skin. Especially when I sat in the sun, pen in hand, and heard hundreds of sheep crammed together on the road behind me, *baa-haa*-ing their way toward a meadow, led by a lonely Irish shepherd.

But it wasn't until day five of our trip—our longest day—that I began to realize what was really happening in my soul, the war between my body and my heart. This was the day we were to attempt Connor's Pass, seven miles straight up a mountain, five miles down and then another twenty or so before we'd reach our lodging for the night. I was already tired and had all but succumbed to the idea that I could not make the trek up the mountain, especially when we awoke to heavy rain. A downpour so hard it washed away any fingernail of confidence or energy I had left. These were the Irish rains we'd been warned about: windy, dark, unending, daunting. The roads would be slick and dangerous, visibility minimal.

Over porridge, tea, and blood sausage, Cearran told the six of us that anyone who didn't think she could make the ride—or didn't want to ride in the rain—could ride with him in his car to the next town. Connor's Pass, he said, was tough on sunny days, let alone rainy ones. I gulped my coffee and was ready to confess. The car option was inviting.

But the younger women among us were not so easily intimidated. Within minutes of finishing their breakfast, they were putting on their rain gear, buttoning up jackets, and filling their water bottles. I glanced from the rain pounding on the window to the light in their faces and wondered if I could do the same. My body was weary, my heart tense. Which should I listen to? Which part of my almost-forty-year-old bones and muscles and soul would get me over the pass?

"You'll never know unless you try," Cearran sang to me. And with no sense of where I was or what I was doing, I watched myself grab my rain jacket and follow my friends to our bikes. As soon as we walked outside, though, we were drenched. This was a flood coming down from the heavens—not a drizzle or a stream, but a flood. Alive. Threatening. Precarious. Instead of recoiling from its impact, two of our team members shouted, reveling in the soaking rain. The August temperature had kept the air warm enough to make the rain surprisingly refreshing. Besides, the young ones said, once we started riding, our bodies would warm up and keep us going. We made a pact to go at our own pace up the pass and wait for each other at the top.

I begged God for more than a few miracles and straddled my bike. Heart pounding, legs aching, rain falling, faith fading.

Apparently, God doesn't seem to mind desperate prayers. I put my bicycle in the lowest possible gear, and the minute I started up Connor's Pass, rain hurling into my face, I felt a gust of wind come from behind me and push me forward. The jolt caught me off guard, and I squeezed the handlebars to steady myself.

That was weird, I thought. I kept pedaling. Back and forth up this narrow mountain road, I pedaled, hearing only the sound of my breathing and the rain splattering on the wet, hard ground. I focused my attention on the few feet ahead of me and kept travers-ing across the road, forming what might have looked like a long *S* to someone flying over in a plane. Every now and then I'd look at the growing incline and the deep green valley below getting smaller and smaller. Or I'd look at the rocky hill beside me and notice the patches of green fade the higher I got. What did I think I was doing?

After the first few miles, fatigue and dampness began taking their toll. I wondered again if I had been hasty or stupid or foolish in my decision to try. I was hardly a kid anymore. Without even time to debate, I felt another gush of wind come from behind me and shove me forward. At least five feet I rode uphill *without* pedaling. I laughed out loud—sheer nervous release. Then I looked up at the hill beside me and saw a thick current of rain shooting out of a huge boulder, water coming *from* the rock. Next to the rock and out of nowhere, five or six snow-white sheep grazed. When they heard my huffing, they lifted their heads and looked at me as if they knew how hard this climb was. I smiled back in response. And not far ahead of me on the road was a low, full cloud, rolling over the ground and leading me upward.

With another push of wind, I sprang forward and I thought, *I'm riding through the Old Testament!* Water pouring from the rock, a cloud to lead this fearful Israelite up the hill, sheep grazing around me, and the wind—oh, the wind—to give me motion. Movement. Wind-propelled. The patience of the Almighty in dealing with doubting, weary, fearful souls. Though my body was spent and my spirit cowardly, the wheels on my bicycle had become my legs, enabling me to see and feel and touch more than I ever could have on my achy, debilitated limbs. No, the Maker of this glorious land had not abandoned me. And never would—no matter how old or young I felt.

By the time I reached the top of Connor's Pass, three of the women were waiting, looking over the edge. A local driver had told them that on a clear day from that point, you could see miles and miles of the coastal line, across valleys and meadows and villages. Too bad today was so cloudy and rainy, he said to them as he drove off. But by the time our last rider friend joined us in the cloister at the top, another miracle happened: the clouds rolled away before us and we *did*—all of us—see the coastal view. We drank in the greens and blues with our eyes, rain dripping off our cheeks, mouths dropped in awe and praise. Silent. Moved—and very high. I stepped away from the edge. Within minutes, the splendor was blocked again when dark, wet clouds rolled back in front of us. No matter. We had seen the view from the top of Connor's Pass.

I took my time going down the mountain; slippery roads and waterfalls made me cautious again. But by the time we reached the valley and a two-hundred-year-old pub in an even older village, I was ecstatic—and relieved. We parked our bikes and went inside for hot soup and chips. Never mind that we still had twenty miles to go that day. In the rain. Along the windy coast.

It was time to dry off and celebrate.

"I love everything that's old: old friends, old times, old manners, old books, old wines."

—HARDCASTLE, in Goldsmith's play *She Stoops to Conquer*

Sunsets never grow old. I watch yellow streaks teasing the sky at the end of this day and I smile. I know what's coming. Soon it will be full of orange and white and gold strokes brushed above the ocean blue, the rewards of a long, full measure of work. But the painting won't last more than a few minutes. It wasn't meant to.

Maybe it's because we can't see many sunsets through the high-rise apartment and office buildings in the city where my husband and I live that I especially love watching it set here at the edge of the sea. Foamy waves roll over changing sandy earth, white gulls glide above, and children grab the last ray of light to play in the water. The wet breeze sprays my arms, washing off dry salty spots and cooling burnt skin. I reach down, grab a shell, and toss it into a wave as it rises and breaks onto the sand. Beyond the surf, I notice the dark blue horizon beginning to blend into the sky like a curtain on a stage, and I suddenly feel the need to applaud. I do. It was a well-made day.

But as the twilight falls and I step back toward the spot where my towel lies, a small burst of pain rushes through my hip—another reminder that the day is not the only thing yielding to the pull of time. I pause for a second to regain my footing. I think of my climbs up previous mountains, of those people who have walked before me, and I feel stronger in my steps. Yes, my bones might be slowing, but cool waters, easy strolls, and rainy memories at least keep me moving ahead. And maybe someday I will even be glad for the privilege of aging. For the dignity of growing…old.

I take one last glance across the sea as I walk toward the road, and the eternity of it surprises me, as if I have never seen it before. I really should start thinking more about heaven.

faded words

(and the legacy I almost lost)

> I thought I could change the world. It took me a hundred years
> to figure out I can't change the world. I can only change Bessie.
> And honey, that ain't easy either.
>
> —BESSIE DELANY, *Having Our Say*

Certainty is a suspicious character to me. I am baffled by those who wink and grin and confidently claim, "What matters most is the direction a person heads in life," or those who put up their hands and tell me, "No, it is what you leave behind—your legacy—that is important."

I confess, when I wake up in the morning, I don't see the lines so easily drawn. I am glad simply to be breathing.

I was four years old the first time I almost died. Most of the kids in our neighborhood had contracted the measles about the same time. Once it ran its course, they were fine. But my measles grew bigger than the others', my mother tells me now, and eventually they turned into the German measles. For some reason, this was more than my four-year-old body could resist.

Early one morning, the story goes, while everyone in our suburban home was still sleeping, my little lungs let out a wail and a holler so loud I'm sure even Mrs. Shanahan, my piano teacher down the street, heard me. The screams rose in volume in direct proportion to the rising temperature in my body, and in a matter of minutes, my mother was distraught, trying to determine what to do with me.

Her own mother had died when my mom was only eleven years old; cancer killed her quickly. My mother spent the next five years—crucial years for girls—with a mean aunt, a bossy big brother, and a father who took new jobs like sailors take trips. Eventually my grandfather remarried and fathered three more children, but the nurturing hand of a parent rarely stroked my mom. Mothering, then, was not necessarily an easy habit for her to pick up. Especially since grief had long been buried in her soul. She was hardly prepared for her baby daughter—of all people—to be the one to call it forth.

But now it threatened to stir anyway. I was hotter than the sun, my body stiff as wood, and the cries from my tiny being were demanding all the world take note of my effort to fight this affliction. My panicked mom called the doctor, who sent over an ambulance, which took me to the doctors at Saint Joseph's Hospital, who hooked me up with IVs, and who then told my mom to relax—as if that were possible for a young mother in 1962 whose only daughter lay stiff and screaming in a bright but sterile room that smelled of chemicals and disinfectant.

I went into a coma sometime before noon. My fever would not subside. By midafternoon the doctor's face turned serious and tired. He was not optimistic. In fact, he told my mother and father to prepare for the worst.

"Your little girl might not make it," he said. Grief poked its head up, and my mom began to cry, her shoulders shivering in terror. My father paced the room where I lay. And for the next three days I stayed in a clinically diagnosed comatose state, tubes running everywhere from my arms to moving hangers, body lying hot and dormant. My mother still considers those some of her darkest days in life.

I, on the other hand, do not remember it at all. What I do recall is waking up and asking the nurse for a grape Popsicle. Sweaty, awake, and confused about what I was doing in this yucky green room, I put the frozen stick to my lips and looked out the window at the boats sailing on the man-made reservoir across from the hospital. I wanted to play.

And I made sure everyone knew. With loud shrill words.

"Back to normal," my mom told the nurses, relaxing her neck a little as she drew a deep breath. I suppose neither of us had fully realized the seriousness of my three-day dance with death. Only after my mother replayed the ordeal to neighbors several times over did she see what could have happened. Because when you think about it, just as no child ever expects to lose a parent, no parent ever expects to lose a child.

What she does expect is to watch her daughter's legs grow longer and her mind grow stronger. She expects to talk with her about shopping, sex, checking accounts, values, and books. A parent, in fact, assumes she will record on glossy paper her child's first swimming lesson, her first date, her college graduation, and her wedding. The two lives, their words, their history are tied together.

So to lose a child would be to lose a legacy, a piece of yourself that plants the heart and veins and eyes of all you are in the earth's memory. It would steal your hope.

Obviously God did not think it time to take my mother's hope by bringing a four-year-old suburban girl to heaven. I think he knew there were too many Popsicle flavors left to try, too many stories left to tell.

And I confess, at that age, I'm sure I wouldn't have wanted to lose that little legacy I had taken four years to build.

"Ships at a distance have every man's wish on board...that is the life of men. Now women forget all those things they don't want to remember, and remember everything they don't want to

forget. The dream is the truth. Then they act and do things accordingly."

—ZORA NEALE HURSTON, *Their Eyes Were Watching God*

There was a time when I knew I wanted to be a mother. I was in my early thirties—I was too busy to notice that wanting before then. Some internal instinct welled up in my soul every time I walked past a child, which was often in the urban neighborhood where I lived in Denver. My apartment was located on a block between a public swimming pool and a park's small lake, so I would frequently watch families picnicking by the water or splashing in the pool's kiddy section. And I would wonder when I might have a child to throw my towel around when she got out of the pool or to make peanut butter sandwiches for when we went to the park.

It was a desire that ached.

But for all the aching, it was a dream that stayed a dream. What happened instead was what always seems to happen in life: the unexpected. My daily walks through the neighborhood turned into years—years that produced essays and articles and friendships while babies and family outings remained in the care of those around me. I grew accustomed to being an aunt or a neighbor and soon realized this was a good direction for me, full and rich and satisfying. I suppose I parented from a distance, even hanging my nephew's coloring pictures on my refrigerator and carrying my neighbors' school photographs in my purse, telling their stories to friends who politely smiled and nodded.

When you reach your forties, though, another instinct kicks in: reality. You listen to the lectures about biological clocks ticking away, and you hear the sermons on investing in the future to build your legacy. And as you listen, you begin to long merely for walks through simple streets and easy answers.

It is a reflective longing.

The first time my husband and I talked about having children—just a month before we married—it was snowing outside. The Hudson River was frozen, and as we drove beside it in my beat-up car, we were wrapped in winter coats and careful words. Our wedding was a few weeks away, and this was an issue that for some reason we both had avoided in most of our conversations about the future. Now, as he confessed his regret in not being a father by his age (forty-five) and his uncertainty of whether it was still what he wanted, I looked at the icy patches scattered across the river. I listened to the quivering in his voice—Australians are rarely used to such winter cold or such vulnerability.

It was not a comfortable discussion. We both knew too well the Christian clichés: the "blessing of a full quiver" or the joys of "training up a child in the way she should go." We reminded each other of friends and family members who had become creative— though exhausted—mothers and fathers. They took their children to the beach, wiped their noses, showed them how to toss a ball, read aloud to them, and prayed with them. We admired their com-

mitment, knowing that each morning they made sure their children were clean and dressed; each afternoon they made sure they
were welcomed and encouraged; each night they made sure they'd
been fed and loved. Parenting, we agreed, must be one of life's most
incredible vocations, requiring all of who you are for most of your
days on earth.

"But does that mean we could or should do it?!" I asked him as
I turned up the window defroster in the little gray car though I
knew it hadn't worked in years. I had to admit as well, that marrying late in life made me question the decision to bear a child at our
ages, wondering how "fair" it would be for her to graduate from
high school when we would be in our late sixties. Plus, with his
involvement in church work and my precarious freelancing career,
could we provide food, clothing, and time for a child? Of course, I
said, looking toward the river that looked colder now through the
foggy windows, I recognized that we were not God, and as friends
liked to remind me, "Sarah and Abraham were pretty old when
they had Isaac." Besides, they also liked to tell me, God never calls
you to something without also providing for you.

We both laughed nervously at the trite sayings as the car in
front of us slowed to avoid a snowy patch in the road.

That, at least, was the easy explanation I offered my husband-
to-be. The other part of the truth was that every time I thought
about being a parent, my muscles collapsed, my mind froze, and
my heart beat faster than it would even in twenty-foot waves on
a hot summer day. Of course I loved children, I reminded this

man who by now was pulling off the river's highway and into the community we would soon call home. He knew how my nephew, nieces, and neighborhood kids delighted my spirit, how I could not imagine anything more miserable than a childless existence.

"But," I said, clapping the cold from my fingers and hearing the volume of my voice rise, "that does not necessarily mean I can imagine having one of my own. Just think what it must feel like being so completely responsible for the well-being of a tiny human life that you cannot sleep or eat or run an errand without first thinking of him?"

I was staring hard now at the man beside me in this freezing car, my eyes wide and not blinking, shoulders trembling from the conversation and the January cold.

We stopped at a red light and decided it might be best to table the discussion for a while, until there wasn't as much stress in our lives or until our car heater got fixed. Marriage itself, my husband-to-be said, would take some time to adjust to, especially for two very independent people. The possibility of parenting could wait. Besides, it might not be in the picture at all, he said, taking my hand in his. "And that's okay," he said gently.

I nodded, my eyes and shoulders calming a bit. Then as we turned the corner, I looked out the foggy window and saw a young mother zipping up the coat of her little boy. She was carrying him down the icy street.

Results from an internet search of Webster's 1828 dictionary:

LEG'ACY, [L. *legatum,* from lego, to send, to bequeath.] A bequest; a particular thing, or certain sum of money given by last will or testament; *Good counsel is the best legacy a father can leave to his child.*

Pronunciation: leg´ uh sE

Function: *noun*

Inflected Form(s): *plural* -cies

Etymology: Middle English *legacie* office of a legate, bequest, from Middle French or Medieval Latin; Middle French, office of a legate, from Medieval Latin *legatia,* from Latin *legatus*

Date: 15th century

1 : a gift by will especially of money or other personal property : BEQUEST

2 : something transmitted by or received from an ancestor or pre-decessor or from the past <the *legacy* of the ancient philoso-phers.

Synonyms: gift, dowry, aid, prize, contribution, bestowal, giveaway, gift horse, heritage.

I was twenty-two years old the second time I almost died—well, sort of died. Throughout my youth, I managed to sidestep any other encounters with my mortality, save an emotional dying here and there when I was sent to the principal's office or when a friend stopped being one. After college I landed a one-year contract teaching and coaching in a Denver suburb, so by summer I was looking for work again. When I was offered a summer position at a girls' camp in Vermont, I saw it as an opportunity to see a part of the country I'd never visited, expand my teaching career, and make enough money until the fall.

What I did not expect was to spend June, July, and August in such a lifeless place.

By June, I was driving my '76 Honda station wagon across the United States and through the Vermont countryside like a boy in adolescence: curious, invincible, and secretly insecure. Camp D for Girls was a Jewish camp that sat on the edge of a small mountain lake known as Lake D. A long thin dock, with canoes and rowboats tied to its side, hung over the northern end of the lake and formed a path to a cluster of twenty or so log cabins. As a young teacher from the West, I had led Bible discussions for high-school students, attended several camps sponsored by youth organizations, and felt familiar with the challenges and strategies of working with kids. I knew little about Jewish culture. And even though the pine trees and mountain lake were reminders to me of Colorado summers long conquered, I was not so sure what I was getting into.

Arlene, the camp director, told me I was the most experienced counselor that summer (which probably said more about the camp than it did about me). Apparently, that's why she put me in charge of fifteen of the oldest girls—campers who had attended Camp D most of their summers while their parents toured Europe without them—and then told me to let her know if I had any "problems" with these kids. Other staff shook their heads at my assignment and warned me to "be careful." Because I was the authority for these teenagers, they cautioned me, I was the enemy.

No wonder. Each morning my task was to wake them up and then direct these "princesses" (as they called each other) to the dining hall, where they served eggs and sarcasm to eight- and nine-year-old girls who had spent the night crying for their mothers or daddies. Next I was to make sure the teenagers washed plates, mopped floors, and showed up again to do the same for lunch and then dinner. It was not a lifestyle these girls were used to; most came from homes where hired maids served their meals and washed their plates. Kitchen duty was hardly the summer fun they had hoped for.

Tension from their orphaned independence and my foreign faith hung every day like the New England humidity: thick, heavy, and silent—the kind of tension that questions even the slightest movement you make. No matter what I said or how I said it—and I pulled out every youth-work strategy I could think of—I could not get inside their world. Each girl seemed resentful of just about everything; worse, their corporate misery created a brick wall no outsider could penetrate. No amount of jokes, prizes, deals, threats, or privileges made any impact on these girls. It didn't help that they already had everything they needed. In fact, these girls had more designer shorts, perfumes, and shoes than they'd ever need for the summer. They had everything, that is, but the one thing they really wanted: a parent's attention. Their mothers and fathers were traveling somewhere across the ocean without them. And these girls were furious about it.

I turned to the only safety I had known myself as a teen: writing. Journal entries and letters west provided a shaky solace during that strange summer of 1982. In between protecting camp meals, keeping canoes right-side up, or preventing craft time from dissolving into a gang fight, I wondered what I was doing in this place and filled pages of my diary discussing such angst. Every time I walked from the dock to the soccer field to the kitchen, I found myself looking over my shoulder, just in case some spoiled child had been pushed a little too hard. *Why had I taken this job again?* I asked myself over and over in letters to friends. *Didn't I know I did not belong here?* I clung to the hope of September when my contract ended, the girls went back to their families, and I could leave this angry place.

One late night in August, while writing in my cabin room and enjoying the only quiet of the day, I was interrupted by hysterical screams down the hall from the room of the "waitresses." I sighed and rolled my eyes. This was not the first night such screams disrupted what might otherwise have been a peaceful summer night. "Disgusting" bugs, pillow fights gone awry, or toothpaste spread across someone's sheets had provoked many a midnight howl, so I was not initially alarmed at the piercing hysteria. I kept writing.

But when I heard several thumps on my door and someone call out, "Jo, you'd better get out here! NOW!" I jumped from my bunk and pulled the knob.

It was Mindy, dark brown hair covering her forehead and glasses like a sheepdog, shoulders heaving back and forth, hands and eyes darting backward and forward. Now I *was* alarmed—this was the ringleader of the rebels, the queen troublemaker among the princesses, the only teenager I had ever met whose vocabulary consisted entirely of four-letter curse words and death threats. Now the short, tough girl standing before me was suddenly young.

Terror has a way of melting marble statues into newborn babies within seconds.

"It's...in...our...room," Mindy managed to whisper between breaths and heaves. I grabbed the closest weapon I could find—a broom—and ran with this fifteen-year-old child to fight whatever IT was. I had no idea what I would do once I got there, especially because my heart was pounding faster and louder than Mindy's was by now. Still, I was the adult here, I told myself; I could be brave.

All fifteen girls were screaming as loud as they could when we arrived, clinging to pillows and cowering beside bunks throughout the cabin. As I told Mindy to stop for a minute to tell me what was the matter, I felt a sudden pinch on top of my head. I ducked instinctively and held up the broom while Mindy let loose a familiar expletive and dove for her pillow. A country bat the size of a designer shoe had somehow gotten inside the cabin and was swooping and flying from rafter to rafter, trying to find an escape. Its black wings formed an eerie *W,* and its constant motion across the cabin was an assault on all our emotions.

I started shaking. I had never seen a bat before, especially this close, and was certain everything I had ever seen about them in the movies was true. It was going to attack me, bite me, fill me with poison, and kill me. I would die in this Jewish girls' camp far from my family and friends in the West, trying to help angry teenage girls who just wanted their mothers to love them so they wouldn't have to act so tough all the time. Then they would pack up my body in a pine casket and ship it by train to Colorado. The girls would take their fancy clothes and stupid crafts home with them and tell their families it had been a pretty dull summer. Nothing very exciting at all. Can't even remember our counselor's name.

Mindy's shrill four-letter words slapped me back into reality, and I yelled for the girls to quit screaming. "Someone open that window over there," I demanded, and the ringleader climbed on the back of another princess and threw open the shutter. Then with a heave she forced the window as high as it would go and jumped back beside the bunk on the floor. I stood up, raised my broom like a flag, and began to punch the bat toward the window. It swooped a bit, my heart stopped, and I dropped beside another princess. Then I raised the broom again and whacked the little wings in the direction of the window like a blindfolded child strikes at a piñata. Within seconds the black blur was out of the cabin and into the darkness of the woods. And just as quickly as it had flown out, the queen leaped toward the window, slammed it down, threw the shutters back in front of it, and jumped back on her bunk. I dropped the broom and collapsed on a bed, hoping to find some air.

"Well, finally, I can get some sleep around here," Mindy proclaimed.

I rubbed my eyes and turned my head slowly toward this thing who had just spoken. Because as quickly as she had dropped to pieces, her marble face had returned. No time to feel. No time to let on that she might be human.

"Yeah, it's about time," another princess chimed in.

"Geez, this place is the pits. When do we get to leave again?"

"Somebody better turn off those #*! lights before I throw something."

"By the way, I'm not getting up in the morning for those brats' breakfast tomorrow. Let 'em get their own meal…"

"Back to normal," I said to no one in particular. With that, I collected my weapon and walked back toward my room to finish my letter, wondering if I was going to survive another month. I had to confess, these young women were beginning to steal my hope.

After many more near-death experiences in tipped canoes, food (and pan) fights, and bat attacks, I arrived at the last day of camp feeling that having survived was nothing short of a miracle.

My Honda was packed, and I could hardly wait to drive off to the safe and familiar roads of my western state. Just as I was turning the ignition, another counselor poked her head in the car window and told me Arlene had organized an awards ceremony. What?! I couldn't believe she might think any child at this camp deserved an award, even if it was just for surviving the three months. As far as I was concerned, Lake D could be thrown into a tin can and stored on a high dusty shelf in my memory, out of reach, out of sight. I was certain I would never be in Vermont ever again.

So when Arlene announced at the awards ceremony that this summer's "humanitarian" award went to the counselor who oversaw the waitresses in the dining room, I looked around the room wondering who she was talking about. Then Mindy threw a marble glance my way, and all the others—campers and counselors and staff alike—followed. Mindy clapped her hands for a second to start a round of applause and then folded her arms defiantly across her chest.

A humanitarian award?! For what? Not killing anyone or letting anyone kill me?

"For showing consistent kindness to all of us at Camp D," Arlene was saying as she handed me a little metal trophy. Kindness? *I just wanted to stay alive,* I thought. But I smiled politely at the acknowledgment and walked quickly back to my car.

The long drive back west made me realize how tired I was. Depleted. Spent from trying to speak a language I never learned.

Discouraged from thinking I would ever make a difference in a teenager's life. I stopped several times along the way to sleep in motels or to nap at rest areas. I could not get enough sleep.

When I finally arrived in Denver, I found a curious letter on the top of my three-month pile of mail. I shook my head as I read the return address: It was from Mindy. I opened it carefully—just in case—as a few photos of us standing by Lake D dropped out of the envelope. And on a lined piece of notebook paper, Mindy had scribbled *me* a letter, telling me she thought I might like these pictures and hoping I'd stay in touch with her. I rubbed my eyes as I read her words again.

I guess the little girl had not forgotten her camp counselor's name after all.

"But words are things, and a small drop of ink,
Falling like dew upon a thought, produces
That which makes thousands, perhaps millions, think."

—LORD BYRON, *Don Juan*, canto 3, stanza 88

The ache to be remembered throbs and pulls on a woman's soul. If it is not children who carry her memory, she will search for other means to confirm her presence on earth.

A few months after my husband and I were married, we drove

to Long Island for a weekend out of the city, hoping the cool spring weather at the beach would bring rest and perspective. As we zipped up jackets and walked along the shore, our conversation turned again to family. We talked about the subject of children, and again we expressed regret and fear—and resolve to leave the ominous privilege of parenting to those younger and more secure. Maybe, we concluded, God would allow us to leave our mark in other ways. Maybe, I whispered as cold drops of the Atlantic sprayed our faces in the breeze, maybe that is the real reason I write: to leave my mark.

And I have been thinking about that ever since, wondering if words and stories—not children—are how I'd be remembered. Partly because I cannot recall a time in my life when I did not write. Not long ago, for instance, when I was required to fill out some forms for a house mortgage, the banker asked me in a most professional manner how long I had been a writer. I replied with the only reasonable answer I could think of: "I was born this way." He did not smile.

Of course, it is one thing to tell a mortgage banker you're a writer or your husband as you walk beside him on the shore; quite a different thing to make such a claim to readers, in a book about fears no less. Some nights I wake up in a cold sweat, hoping my husband will offer some profound reminder of my purpose in life because all I can think to ask him is, Why couldn't I have been a plumber? Or a baker? Why did I end up in work that feels as risky as, well, jumping off a boat into the middle of the ocean? Of course, it is not simply absolute terror I feel for the unknown life in the water below; no, it is fear of being spotted from the ship—that is, of being identified as an "important writer"—and then, alas, forgotten.

Abandoned at sea.

Faded words.

Of course I am aware that more normal people become principals or chefs, others bankers or social workers, actors or clerks, mechanics or attorneys, pastors or photographers. They leave their prints on the world in a thousand different forms, but I have discovered since that weekend talk with my husband on the shore, few people seem to think about what they'll leave behind when their social working and photographing and banking have ended.

Some say they only hope to be happy or to have loved their children well; others confess they want merely to have achieved their goals in this life without worrying about the next one. And one faith-filled friend told me recently that it never occurred to her what sort of legacy she might have; her mind is so filled with the hope of heaven in the world beyond that she does not consider what earthly mark she will make. Maybe that is because she works with five- and six-year-old special-needs children whose emotional agonies and shattered homes are often more than any human can bear. Heaven—the place of no more tears—is a much better option for them, for her. Forget the idea of a legacy on this planet;

it seems a ridiculous luxury even to consider for those merely hoping to survive.

And though I believe heaven is as real as the computer in front of me, I confess that my vision of it is regularly overshadowed by the earthly elements surrounding me. I live in the confined world of printed memories, where the words and faces and feelings of today distract me from the streets of gold, making heaven seem far away. Like a trip you plan and save for someday in the future—though you're secretly afraid you'll never get on the boat. And you're even more afraid that religious people will question whether you ever had a ticket to begin with for having admitted such a thing. Legacy, to them, seems to be counting the number of souls saved at the altar of their ministry.

So I wrap the knuckles of my shaky faith around language that, whether I like it or not, stays caught like a bat between the rafters in a windowless page. And I write. In our apartment. At a friend's house in Long Island. On an airplane or in the subway or at a café. Anywhere, really, I can jot down an idea or something I've just witnessed. I guess I keep writing because I do think more about what I will leave behind than where I hope to go. And because writing is both who I am while living and what I do to earn one. In many ways, it is how I make sense of this world and perhaps how the world will make sense of me.

John Steinbeck said, "In utter loneliness a writer tries to explain the inexplicable.... The writer must believe that what he is doing is the most important thing in the world. And he must hold to this illusion even when he knows it is not true." I don't know exactly when this illusion started for me. As Steinbeck suggested, it must have developed during the lonely times of my life, when written words became my refuge and friend, a necessary companion for growing up in a family that admittedly did not always know how to communicate very well with each other. I swallowed words whole any way I could get them: in books, in songs, in diaries, in stories, in television shows, in theater, and in magazines. Whether beside swimming pools, mountain rivers, or backyard benches, reading or writing made me *feel* connected, like I belonged. Somehow words knew to cry for me when I didn't know how or to cheer me on when I was going in the right direction. I see now that sentences, books, and stories were most of the courage I had, gifts with lasting influence.

When I was ten years old, for example, I was certain I would become an Olympic athlete. Some important person—I think it was a librarian—gave me a book called *This Life I've Lived,* the autobiography of Babe Didrikson Zaharias. Alone in my room, I would turn page after page to watch her defy cultural standards and become one of our country's greatest female athletes, winning Olympic gold medals in the javelin and the 80-meter hurdles in 1932 and setting world records in both. I watched her as she pitched in spring training for major and minor league baseball teams, as she toured with a basketball team, and as she walked the greens of her career as a professional golfer, helping even to found the LPGA.

I ached when I read about Babe's battle with cancer and how it killed her in 1956, two years before I was born. But because of touching Babe's story on thin-bound paper, I wanted to be an athlete. With my book safely beside my bed and until there was no more light outside, I would practice hurdling my neighbor's bushes the way Babe did; I'd pound the pavement with my brother's basketball the way Babe did. Her words convinced me that if she could run with the best of them, I could at least try.

When I turned eleven, though, I changed my mind and my reading. I decided that instead of being an Olympic athlete, I would become a famous detective. If Nancy Drew could solve every mystery on the planet as a young girl—as her hard, blue-and-gold-covered books proclaimed—why couldn't I? Each new story in the Nancy Drew Mystery series gave me new sleuthing episodes as well, sending me into dark basements, abandoned fields, and my mother's kitchen, where I experimented with flour fingerprint techniques and food-coloring formulas.

The beauty of books is that they offer an array of identities. By the time I was thirteen, my detective investigations turned to other adventures (plus my mom got tired of my kitchen messes). Other pages from other books gave me other stories and lands, the wide-open prairie where the house of Laura Ingalls Wilder sat; the urban streets where African-American children walked to school; the fields and trails of heroes in history whose lives changed everyone they touched. I found roaming through paper worlds as necessary to my survival as rain on Wilder's prairie or street smarts for urban teens.

But I never expected to *be* a writer. Yes, I read the expeditions of others in book after book, and I wrote in my diary or journal about every emotion I had, every feeling I felt. In the basement family room or in my bedroom, I'd swap between writing a poem in my diary or reading a chapter in whatever book I had checked out from the library. I still do. It did not, however, occur to me that this could be a career to pursue when I grew up, and therefore, one way the earth might remember me. After all, what suburban girl in the 1960s ever dreamed of becoming anything but a mother, a housewife, or a teacher? These were the safe futures, comfortable and predictable.

But I don't think writing is ever safe. And after many conversations along many shores with kindred souls, I have come to believe that writing is double-edged fear: You fear having your words, your thoughts, and your stories read, but you fear more that they will never be read at all.

"All streams flow into the sea, yet the sea is never full. To the place the streams come from, there they return again. All things are wearisome, more than one can say. The eye never has enough of seeing, nor the ear its fill of hearing. What has been will be again, what has been done will be done again; there is nothing

new under the sun. Is there anything of which one can say, 'Look! This is something new?' It was here already, long ago; it was here before our time. There is no remembrance of men of old, and even those who are yet to come will not be remembered by those who follow."

—ECCLESIASTES 1:7-11

I was thirty-eight years old the third time I almost died. The winter before I met my husband in England, I agreed to join friends for a ski trip to a state I hadn't been in sixteen years: Vermont. At first I was reluctant to go; my previous (and only) encounter with the New England state was less than inviting. But I also recognized that my hip was not as strong as it once was, so I was not sure how the winter slopes would treat me. The more I thought about it, the more the combination of Vermont and skiing seemed potentially lethal.

Still, "the eye never has enough of seeing," especially when the assurance from good friends makes you believe that an experience might not be as bad as you think.

The fact that there was a blizzard in New York the Friday afternoon we were to leave should have been warning enough. But Colorado-winter confidence runs deep, and I was hardly troubled by the icy roads and heavy white flakes that flew into our windshield. My friend Andrea decided to drive first. She, too, seemed virtually unaffected by the winter storm, having built her confidence from many snowy battles during college days in Syracuse.

Besides, she had made this trip many times before to visit her brother and sister-in-law, so she assured me it was an easy five-hour drive. Halfway to Vermont the two of us were to meet other friends for dinner, so we crossed the East River out of the city and settled in for the drive north.

What we hadn't expected was traffic. Caution sat behind every steering wheel, and car after car clogged the wintry interstate like boulders do mountain streams. Andrea shifted into second gear as we slowed to join the other cars crawling along Interstate 95. Once the sun went down so did the temperatures, freezing both the lanes and what little confidence remained in the drivers around us. We moved at an even slower pace. But with the headlights throwing a dreamy light on the road and the wipers pounding back the snow in 2/4 rhythm, we inched along the winter road more absorbed in our conversation than in the conditions around us.

What provokes fear for some is second nature for others. We forget, though, how slippery such assurance can be.

By the time we crossed the Connecticut state line, the traffic began to thin out. Some cars got off the interstate while others continued their crawling speed. Andrea left both as she shifted into third, sped up to about forty-five miles per hour and moved into the passing lane, talking with me as if the world outside were invisible. The heavy snow against the window inspired skiing stories and winter memories, and we talked and laughed and listened with Friday-afternoon freedom. We'd be in Vermont before long.

But it is true what they say about near-death experiences: Time seems frozen on the road while you watch your life stagger out in front of you.

Our car's back tire must have caught dark ice as we changed lanes. Andrea pumped the brakes and turned the wheel, but as she did, it was clear the car was going where it wanted to. We swerved over into the middle lane and then farther across into the third lane, forming the lower loop of a figure eight in our tracks. Gliding. Circling. Turning almost completely around. Snow smashing against the window. Cars on both sides of us. Ice on every part of the surface. Terror squeezing every piece of air from inside the car.

"Oh, Jesussssss," burst from my mouth, though I don't know how I managed to make a sound. Suddenly, faces attached to floating bodies formed in the headlights: my mom, dad, nieces, students, friends, nephew, neighbors. They all flew out in front of our car—some waving, some dancing, some just staring like a deer while I tried desperately to push them out of the way. Within seconds, snow, faces, lights, woods, all formed a black blur, and I cowered in the passenger seat, clinging to my pillow, gulping each breath.

The conversation Andrea and I had had was now all screams and shouts. We skidded across the three-lane interstate and over the center shoulder of the road, circled into the ditch that separated the two directions of traffic, and collided with a short metal guardrail that apparently had been built for such crashes as these. It caught the back bumper of our car, ripped it off completely and threw it into the road. And with a forty-five-mile-per-hour heave, we spun down the little hill and into the rail again once, then twice, and stopped as suddenly as we had started, jerking us forward, then backward. Headlights faced oncoming traffic. Wipers still beat against the glass in 2/4 rhythm. Ignition dead. Snow thrashing. Bodies shocked.

Silence now blew through the car, the kind that comes when you suddenly feel cold and alive though you know you should probably be neither, the kind that makes you feel small and indebted and glad at the same time. We both stared at the white flakes still dropping into the window. Cars swirled by us, either unaware of what had just happened to us or unable themselves to stop on the icy road. I cleared my throat (though there was nothing really to clear), loosened the grip on my pillow, and raised my shoulders a little higher as if there was something else I should see. And then Andrea started to cry, not because her body hurt. Neither of us had moved an inch during the icy ride and had no injuries from the crash. No, my friend began to release every drop of fear and terror—and awe—that had followed us across three lanes of interstate without hitting another car, down a shallow ditch without flipping over, spinning us completely around without colliding with anything but some flexible metal, leaving us sitting in silence, watching the snow fall and wondering why God had chosen to let us live. I trembled with her tears.

Then I unfastened my seat belt, patted Andrea's shoulder to make sure she was okay, and got out of the car. I walked in snowy darkness around to the driver's seat as Andrea slid over. The car's ignition amazingly turned over, so I backed the car around and merged slowly with the traffic.

Now it was my turn to drive. Maybe Vermont would be nice after all.

" 'Well Done,' said Aslan in a voice that made the earth shake. Then Digory (the son of Adam) knew that all the Narnians had heard those words and that the story of them would be handed down from father to son in that new world for hundreds of years and perhaps forever. But he was in no danger of feeling conceited for he didn't think about it at all now that he was face to face with Aslan. This time he found he could look straight into the Lion's eyes. He had forgotten his troubles and felt absolutely content."

—C. S. LEWIS, *The Magician's Nephew*

(from the Chronicles of Narnia)

If you are given the luxury of looking over your shoulder at the people you have affected, at the work you have accomplished, you know it is a little like looking over the ocean bay you just swam across. You recognize the places where you wondered if you were going to make it; your muscles ached, the tide was strong, and your eyes stung from the salty water. But then you point to the sites where you felt a surge of life rise within you and you kicked and breathed in a rhythm that felt right and full. Both were part of the swim, and both got you here.

Last month my husband and I celebrated our first anniversary. We went to a fancy restaurant on Fifty-first Street, light snowflakes dropping around us, winter cold patting our cheeks. We sat at a table by a cozy window as people in long wool coats hurried by, walking around icy patches on the road. Over wine and salmon steak, my husband and I talked of ocean walks, tired bays, and river drives. It was a year of changing tides, we agreed, that both exhausted and strengthened us for the road ahead. Parts of who we were had died along the way; parts came alive in ways that we had always hoped they would. Parts, of course, hadn't even begun to be explored.

When we sipped our coffee after dinner and walked into the winter darkness, I think we entered year number two feeling hopeful and indebted and glad. Marriage, I realized, is much more of a process than an accomplishment.

I think the same is true of legacies. Whether they're words in a book, movements in a society, wills in a family, or children in a lifetime, somehow they slide their way into history's vault and mark a page that changes and builds and restores this world in ways only they could. Perhaps some even blaze a trail that takes us beyond this earth, to a heavenly land where children never cry for their parents, adults never worry about their futures, and lovers never fear what they shall leave behind.

Still, like Zora Neale Hurston wrote, "There is no agony like bearing an untold story inside you." And so a few weeks after our anniversary, I rode my bicycle past the reservoir at Central Park. Though the streets were clear and dry, the park was covered with snow. Winter branches were barren but waved like fingers toward the sky. The sun sparkled across the frozen lake and beyond it; families sent happy, bundled children down sleds and slippery saucers. As I pedaled just beyond the lake, I caught the laughter of one child in particular: shrill, delighted, demanding. She reveled in the white playground and danced in the snowy mounds. Over and over she laughed, and then as she rode down the hill with her mother, a sound came from her little mouth like one I had never heard before in all my life: "Mommy!"

My soul throbbed. Then it ached. And I kept riding.

faith crossing

I merely took the energy it takes to pout and wrote some blues.

—Duke Ellington

I think I have been learning about faith as long as I have lived in fear. Maybe longer.

To begin with, I believed as a little girl that my mom and dad could make juice and cereal appear each morning on the kitchen table, though I didn't know how they managed it. There were times I was afraid of the dark, but I still felt certain a light would go on once I flicked a switch. I accepted the fact that our house would be warm in winters and that our refrigerator's freezer could turn Kool-Aid into flavored ice each hot summer. I remember the junior-high home economics class that showed me how to make a white fluffy substance from separating an egg, and the skiing instructors who told me that if I pointed my skis straight down the mountain, they would take me that way—something about gravity's pull.

Yes, I believed. Early on. Because that's what humans do: They believe. Every time I tied up my ice skates and wobbled (albeit apprehensively) onto frozen water, I believed. Each time I plopped a seed in the dirt of our backyard garden or whenever I swallowed a vitamin or a green vegetable, I guess I believed then too. Most children, I suppose, live in a world of assumptions and trust and certainty. And if they are lucky—that is, if sin or dismay or selfishness has not first stolen their wonder—such faith grows up with them as they get older.

I felt that wonder when a college friend once pointed at the wind one autumn day as we walked to class—leaves swirling around in circles, plastic grocery bags and broken twigs jumping down the sidewalk. We stopped and "watched the wind" for five minutes. We were smiling, silent. And I knew again that there was something invisible about faith. A power that moves things though you cannot see it. A mystery that invites your heart's response though your eye sees nothing.

Of course, the same could be said of fear. Whenever I am afraid, it is because I am also believing in something unseen, and like faith, fear, too, requires an agile imagination. Both seem to have a way of growing bigger depending on how much attention you give them, although one seems fed by truth and goodness while the other is fanned by worry and dreaded what-ifs. Maybe, though, facing fears shouldn't be nearly as exciting as finding faith; maybe we should reduce fears altogether to lowercase status in our lives, while Finding Faith gets capitalized. Maybe we should even read lowercase fears as prepositional phrases, that is, as those little words that really help us understand their relationship to the subject of the sentence, the Proper Noun. A Person. Truth.

Sort of like jumping into the sea though your stomach is as jittery as the boat, and you call on God out of sheer absolute desperation though you feel anything but spiritual. You feel fear, in fact. Everywhere. But somehow once your skin is submerged in the water, that same fear melts into a fear of God, and it grips you, holds you close, keeps you safe. Makes you new. And your fear—of water, of men, of loneliness, of different people, of being disabled or forgotten—dissolves like ice cubes on a hot summer day. You hardly notice the change, but you drink it up and thirst for more. This, too, like faith, is a gift. Coming from the One who knew before you did that to soothe your soul was his job, not yours. Yours was to jump.

Someone told me once that the original functions of fear were to warn of danger and to protect vulnerable creatures from a threatening attack. That is probably true. But I think fear was also meant to push us overboard—arms flailing, legs kicking, eyes stinging—so that we could be, have to be, rescued. Saved.

And how can we be saved?

Through a story, I think. A sacred one. A lifeline of words and symbols and themes. Merging our stories with a greater one. Yes, the stories remind us that someone else has gone across the lake, that someone else is steering the ship. Or that we have already been in this place before and it is time to move on. Together.

Stories keep us moving. They feed our faith.

"We make an idol out of our fear and call it God."

—INGMAR BERGMAN

A month before our first anniversary, my husband and I sat in a plane for fifteen or so hours and flew across the Pacific. It was Christmastime, and we were heading south—way south—to visit his family in Australia. We were taking our first trip together to his homeland, and to be honest, I was nervous about walking through his memories, meeting his lifelong friends, and living in this new moment called "in-laws."

Even people with shaky faith, however, find that *home* has a mysterious way of redefining itself, of driving your fears away in flight, like you do pigeons in the park. A hug, a cup of tea, and an old, soft chair can make you feel you've been in this kitchen before, even though you never have.

So my definition of home expanded again this past Christmas as I exchanged gifts, "prawns on the barbie," locally grown mangoes, and stories with my new family. We walked along the beaches that have made the Sunshine Coast famous, and we strolled through pages of photo albums that have made—in part—my husband's identity. We swam in the ocean, rode along the coast, and shopped for Vegemite and brand-name jeans that my husband cannot get in the U.S. And we filled our lungs with the fresh salty breeze.

I had not celebrated Christmas in the ocean sun for a long time.

Noosa Heads, the town where my husband's family lives, is about six hundred miles north of Sydney, about where North Carolina would be if you were looking at a map of Australia as if it were the United States. In fact, both countries are equal in size, yet the entire population of the land down under equals the number of those living in the New York City area. Density, in other words, is not a problem in Australia, and space and nature—or "the bush"—are normal requirements for living.

It is not uncommon, then, for Aussies to feel the land inside their souls, to feel its pull and call and life within theirs. It is less common, of course, for former-suburbanite-turned-city-girls to do the same. But I was about to.

"If you begin with certainties, you will end in doubts. But if you're content to begin with great doubts, you will end in certainties."

—FRANCIS BACON, "The Advancement of Learning"

My father-in-law booked us on a tourist bus to explore a place called Fraser Island. Ever since my husband and I met in England,

I had heard the stories of Fraser Island from him, admired his photographs of the sandy island, and heard his passion for its remarkable beauty. So, long before I visited, I already knew that Fraser Island was southern Queensland's proudest possession, the world's greatest sand mass, a natural phenomena of miles and miles of beach and sand sculpted by ocean winds that apparently took more than 400,000 years to create. The island's center is home to astonishing freshwater "dune" lakes and tropical rain forests, even though the entire foundation of the island is sand.

I had heard all these descriptions before, but just as the same is true with faith, a place is never your own until your feet touch its soil and your nose breathes its air.

And so before the sun rose one Monday morning, I put on my swimsuit, grabbed a towel and a T-shirt, and joined my husband and his dad on a four-wheel-drive monster bus. There was not an inch of blue sky in sight, and though it was still dry when we woke up, the forecast called for rain. All day. Before we left Noosa Heads, the clouds let go of their waters, just as a few more family members—sister, brother-in-law, nephew—climbed aboard the bus. We headed north by way of the bush: Cooloola National Park, to be exact. Through fields, woods, and meadows, we drove along single-lane roads in the steady rain, slowing every now and then to watch a mob of eastern gray kangaroos running away from our intrusive bus. They'd freeze at the sight of us, prick up their ears at the threat of danger, and then disappear into the woods. My face pressed hard against the rainy window to catch a glimpse of the handsome animals, and I felt like I was living inside a National Geographic documentary.

By midmorning the rain pounded harder against the glass, and I wrapped my arms inside my T-shirt and towel to stay warm. Soon our bus turned onto a long, colorful beach that sits on the edge of the South Pacific. As I saw where we were going, I could feel the inside of my mouth suddenly dry up. No road, no highway, just a sandy shore where our bus driver took us just inches from the breaking waves. It is one thing to drive beside kangaroos in the bush, quite another to drive *beside* the ocean. I sank lower in my cushioned seat and grabbed the armrest as I watched the white choppy sea crash onto the sand, the bus shifting and darting around the water line like a child chasing waves. I had never done anything at a beach but walk along it, so this four-wheel bouncy ride was a bit like going from the beginners to the expert class in a matter of seconds. I wondered if I belonged there.

I found a silent prayer and held my gaze on the breaking white foam. And I swallowed. A lot.

Around noon I was relieved when the bus pulled onto a huge ferry that would take us across a bay to Fraser Island. On sunny days, my husband told me, dolphins would swim beside the ferry, diving and jumping and entertaining the tourists. If we were lucky, today we might see a few, he said. Even in the rain. So I pressed my face against the ship's glass window and tried to see them. All I saw were choppy waves. Cyclonic weather, someone said.

On the other side of the inlet, we boarded the monster bus

again, drove off the ferry and began the tour around the "world's largest sand mass." Again, we drove across the beach as if it were a highway next to the waves—the ocean was at king tide—and again, my mouth got dry. (King tide, my husband told me, is a flood tide, full, high, heavy. It happens when the moon is full and pulls the water higher than normal, happening only a few times a year.)

An ocean's power, I see now, is both mesmerizing and forbidding; though the constancy of the waves paints an alluring and lively scene, it is nonetheless a force that you know could easily flip your life—and the bus you're riding in—upside down. You watch it like an athlete would observe an opponent. So you can be ready. Just in case.

We drove on Fraser Island's shore for many miles, and I got lost in my thoughts. It had been a long, strange relationship I'd had with water—avoiding, wading, swimming, canoeing, fearing, admiring—and I was still not quite sure why I kept visiting its shores. I sighed and stared for a long time at God's moving depth. As I did, a peculiar thing began to happen: The longer I looked out the window at the white caps of the sea, the more I felt like I was noticing every detail of a beautiful painting. Gray and blue strokes curved up and down, green and white brushes angled forward, calling forth from me that unexplainable but quiet joy that an elegant piece of art always evokes in your soul. I relaxed my grip on the armrest. And I hummed.

The rain beat down on both the sand and the ocean, and the more I became familiar with it, the more I found myself feeling some of my husband's awe for this place. Eventually we left the beach, slowed down and turned into a lush path that took us to the center of the island. Now rain dropped on long, thin, green triangles like icicles that sparkled and glistened against the colors. Trees hung over the sandy path, making a tunnel out of the branches and leaves and fingerlike blades. Vines draped across the road connected from huge tree trunks that stood proud and firm like the Aborigines who once inhabited this island. On some of the trees, our bus driver said, you could even see marks where men had carved the bark out in single sheets to make roofs. Plant life, a few animals, and insects all shared this strange sandy place and echoed a life that was both eerie and inviting.

My feet were starting to touch the soil of Fraser.

"We join spokes together in a wheel but it is the center hole that makes the wagon move. We shape clay into a pot but it is the emptiness inside that holds whatever we want. We hammer wood for a house but it is the inner space that makes it livable. We work with being but non-being is what we use."

— L A O - T Z U , from the New York City subway ad series

Poetry in Motion

When our driver parked the monster at the edge of another sandy path and began telling us about Lake McKenzie, I was by now eager for another layer of this sandy story. The lake—one of the oldest of the island's forty dune lakes—had been created when organic material cemented the sand in a wind-formed depression. Strong prevailing winds tossed sand around in spits and perched it firmly in the center. Scientists say that the sand filtered the water, ridding it of any aluminum compounds and leaving the water crystal clear and miraculously clean. Apparently the small quantities of nutrients act as natural purifiers, and because of its filtered purity, high acidity, and low levels of chemical nutrients, the lake also has very few fish or other aquatic creatures. Most cannot tolerate this environment. In other words, our burly driver told us, "You won't find softer or purer water anywhere. It's only mildly acidic and it'll polish your jewelry, and soften your skin if you go swimming in it."

My husband's family was out of the bus in minutes, hurrying down the sandy path while holding beach towels over their heads as umbrellas. I did not follow them so quickly. The rain was falling harder than it had in the green tunnel, and although the driver's tale had been an interesting one, I could not imagine how a little lake on a sandy hill in the middle of the ocean could be worth a soaking. Even if it was clean and pure.

Faith can be like that. You're never quite sure what you're in for, though you do suspect it will require work to get there. It is a choice to believe beyond what you see.

So after I confessed my anxiety aloud to a nearly empty bus and realized my husband and his family knew something about Lake McKenzie that I did not, I grabbed my towel and jumped out of the monster. Sand slid softly through my toes as I walked toward the path. Cold rain fell hard on my arms and head. It was hard now even to see the Lake McKenzie sign with the arrow pointing down the path. A few tourists ran past me, laughing as a few teenagers coming back from the lake grumbled something about "the stupid weather." I shivered in the green shower—shiny, thin blades and sharp branches poking me—but I kept walking.

Farther down the trail, I noticed tree trunks gnarled like old hands, bushes spiked with jagged cones, and footprints in the wet—but mud-free—sand as different from the beaches back home as the forest around me. But I also noticed that no flowers were growing next to the bushes, no birds were sitting on the branches. In fact, no other colors but greens and browns and whites painted this place at all. Only the pounding rain that hung over this trail like a canopy offered any explanation for the absence of such usual island friends.

But Fraser Island and Lake McKenzie are not like other islands and lakes.

I breathed in the moisture, dropped back my head, and closed my eyes for a second. Water dropped on my eyelids and sand tickled my feet. And for a firm, reassuring moment, the details of my beautiful ocean painting spread across my mind, piercing my soul again, and making me suddenly glad not to be sitting next to that armrest.

I walked a few more yards, and the trail ended at the base of a white beach. At first, the white sand took me back to Colorado snow—milky, quiet, untouched. But I could not look for long on the snowy sand before Lake McKenzie itself demanded my eye. Rain was dancing sweet waltzes across the dark-blue glass, wind calming ripples across the surface. I held my hand out over my eyes to help me see the other side of this lake, but I could not. To the left of the lake sat another forest-green ridge and a mirror of it on the right. But in front of me, I saw no end: just smooth blue water, miraculously clean, far, far before me.

This was not what I expected. I ran over to the white bark of a tall tree and stood under it, hoping it might shelter me from the rain. Beach towels hung over a few of its shorter branches, and a pile of T-shirts and shorts lay around it. I glanced from the pile to the lake and saw not more than fifty yards from this tree that my seventy-year-old father-in-law was swimming laps in the lake. My sister-in-law was springing in and out of the water like a dolphin might. And then I saw my husband, standing with his chest out of the water, waving at me, smiling.

He was inviting me to come for a swim.

"Hope, like faith, is nothing if it is not courageous; it is nothing if it is not ridiculous."

—THORNTON WILDER, *The Eighth Day*

What was he thinking?

Didn't my husband know I was already cold and wet? Hadn't

he and his dad and sister seen all the other tourists who had gone back to the bus by now? Didn't they notice the dark skies above them? Why were they swimming in the rain, for heaven's sake? Who *were* these people?

I shook my head hard in his direction to dismiss the idea of any childish thoughts, wrapped my towel tight around my shoulders, and planted my feet. I could be stern. Then my husband stopped smiling, dropped back into the clear water, and starting swimming to catch up to his dad. His sister did more jumps and dives while his father swam more laps. My husband waved to me a few more times as the rain kept dancing around him. And I stood for ten more minutes under that white tree on the white soft sand, watching my new family swim in Lake McKenzie. As if I were watching a film. Surreal. Irrational. Ridiculous.

Until I couldn't stand it any longer. Fear always has a hard time arguing with Faith. Something about lowercase status.

I let out a wail and hollered, "Aw, what the heck?" Then I threw my towel into the pile, pulled off my T-shirt, and ran. Straight ahead. Into the cleanest, purest, softest water in the oldest dune lake on the biggest sand mass in the South Pacific. And I swam.

I jumped toward my husband, who by now was smiling again and laughing at me, and I darted up and back into the water as if I were a dolphin. I kicked and paddled and slapped that water like a child who's always wanted to swim and yet wasn't allowed to before now. I held my breath and swam along the bottom, eyes wide open, not stinging, as if I were the first person to discover this plant-less lake. I jumped up, dove under, and threw back my head to catch raindrops on my eyelids as I did the backstroke.

And then I sprang toward the man who had first told me of this place, the man whom I had fought with and dreamed with and married, the one who made me believe I could be loved. I hung around his neck, inches from his handsome face, and we paddled around the cleansing water in the rain and laughed and looked and kicked until his father told us the bus was getting ready to go. But by now the lake had actually become warmer than it had been standing on the beach under the tree in the rain. And I did not want to get out.

The bus driver was right, though: my wedding ring *was* shinier after I went swimming.

"There are things, say in learning to swim or to climb, which look dangerous and aren't. Your instructor tells you it's safe. You have good reason from past experience to trust him. Perhaps you can even see for yourself, by your own reason, that it is safe. But the crucial question is, will you be able to go on believing this when you actually see the cliff edge below you or actually feel yourself unsupported in the water? You will have no rational grounds for disbelieving. It is your senses and your imagination that are going to attack belief. Here, as in the New Testament, the conflict is not between faith and reason but between faith and sight.

We can face things which we know to be dangerous if they don't look or sound too dangerous; our real trouble is often with things we know to be safe but which look dreadful. Our faith in Christ wavers not so much when real arguments come against it as when it looks improbable—when the whole world takes on the desolate look which really tells us much more about the state of our passions and even our digestion than about reality."

—C. S. LEWIS, "Religion: Reality or Substitute?"

Christian Reflections

The rains never let up that day on Fraser Island. I was soggy in my seat the rest of the time—we all were—but it didn't really matter. The fresh water had removed for the moment a few of the impurities that had clogged our souls.

After Lake McKenzie, our four-wheel monster took us to a big lodge just off of the island's shore where we gorged ourselves on hot pasta, salad, and tea. (Why do such heroic encounters with nature always make you so hungry?) When we gulped the last of our tea, we climbed back on the bus and drove again around the island, next to the ocean, across on the ferry, and then along the beach toward Noosa Heads. We saw orange and red rocks, scores of soaked campers, and waves that never stopped chopping the sea but never stopped painting beautiful, peaceful pictures. God's art.

The sun came out the next day and the next and all the rest of our stay on the Sunshine Coast with my husband's family. No more rain. But my husband and I returned to New York a little softer from our Lake McKenzie dip, a little calmer in our hearts, and a little more connected to each other in the faith—and in the stories—we shared.

I do not pretend at the end of this book that I will never have another fear the rest of my days on earth—or that I will never doubt the direction I am walking—because fears do not go away even when our souls have jumped overboard, even when we turn toward the One who stills the waters. They are not suddenly exorcised when we call out to him because, of course, we do not stop being human. I think it is simply that we no longer worship them. Instead we stare straight into the face of Truth, riveted by his beauty, so that no shadow, no fear can distract us. Yes, we take our shaky hand of faith—fears and all—and hold on even tighter to his. We trust. We ask the Christ who painted the waves if he will become the artist of our faith, the object of our devotion. And we grab on as he throws out the lifeline, "Let not your heart be troubled, neither let it be afraid."

My husband told me that some spiritual person actually counted the number of references in the Bible (both in Greek and Hebrew) where the phrases "fear not" or "peace be with you" appear. The person concluded there are 366 places with such words—one for each day of the year, including leap year. I do not know if this is really true, but I want it to be. However many times that phrase appears, I know from this place where I now sit as a middle-aged woman who has tried to listen that it comes not as an overwhelming, surreal command, but as an invitation to relation-ship, to come to the water.

Because fear, when we decide to believe it or capitalize it in our hearts, paralyzes us, leaving us scarred and isolated and really, really lonely. But when our fears are woven into the sacred story, we enjoy a gracious friendship, a family even, and we walk down a stirring, exhilarating path. Together.

Sort of like the time I was five, maybe eight years old, and I had a nightmare. I must have screamed or cried because soon my bedroom door opened slowly and a soft, thin light from the hall-way drifted in. My mom walked quietly in and sat on the edge of my bed. She rubbed my back, brushed the hair out of my eyes, and sat there until my eyes got heavy and sleepy.

And I was not afraid anymore.

And so it is when the gentle presence of Faith sits on the edge of our bed, brushing the fear out of our eyes, whispering that everything will be all right. We get rest for tomorrow. It is the best kind of bedtime story imaginable, and we wake up the next morn-ing humming the lullaby we must have heard while we slept:

Rock of Ages, cleft for me,
Let me hide myself in Thee;
Let the water and the blood,
from Thy wounded side which flowed,
Be of sin the double cure,
save from wrath and make me pure.

Not the labors of my hands
Can fulfill Thy law's demands;
Could my zeal no respite know,
Could my tears forever flow,
All for sin could not atone;
Thou must save and Thou alone.

Nothing in my hand I bring,
Simply to Thy cross I cling;
Naked, come to Thee for dress,
Helpless, look to Thee for grace,
Foul, I to the fountain fly,
Wash me, Savior, or I die!

While I draw this fleeting breath,
When my eyes shall close in death,
When I soar to worlds unknown,
See Thee on Thy judgment throne,
Rock of Ages, cleft for me,
Let me hide myself in Thee.

Was it not you who dried up the sea,
the waters of the great deep,
who made a road in the depths of the sea
so that the redeemed might cross over?

—ISAIAH 51:10

bibliography

The following books have fed me plentiful portions of creative courage as I've tried to confront life's fears. I list them here for you, trusting they will nourish you for the journey as well.

Benson, Robert. *Between the Dreaming and the Coming True: The Road Home to God.* San Francisco: HarperCollins, 1996.

Bradbury, Ray. *Fahrenheit 451.* New York: Ballantine Books, 1953.

Buechner, Frederick. *Telling Secrets: A Memoir.* San Francisco: Harper-Collins, 1991.

Booth, Wayne. *The Art of Growing Older: Writers on Living and Aging.* Chicago: University of Chicago Press, 1992.

Coles, Robert. *The Call of Stories: Teaching and Moral Imagination.* Boston: Houghton Mifflin, 1989.

Dillard, Annie. *The Writing Life.* New York: HarperPerennial, 1989.

Dodd, Caley. *Dynamics of Intercultural Communication,* Third Edition. Dubuque, Iowa: Wm. C. Brown Publishers, 1991.

Grolier Multimedia Encyclopedia. Novato, Calif.: Mindscape.com, 1997.

Hurston, Zora Neale. *Their Eyes Were Watching God.* Audio book tape read by Ruby Dee. New York: HarperCollins, 1991.

L'Engle, Madeleine. *Walking on Water: Reflections on Faith and Art.* Wheaton, Ill.: Harold Shaw, 1980.

Lee, Harper. *To Kill a Mockingbird.* New York: Harper and Row, 1960.

Lewis, C. S. *The Magician's Nephew.* New York: HarperTrophy, 1955.

———. *The Quotable Lewis.* Edited by Wayne Matindale and Jerry Root. Wheaton, Ill.: Tyndale, 1989.

———. *The Voyage of the Dawn Treader.* New York: HarperTrophy, 1955.

Mathewes-Green, Frederica. *At the Corner of East and Now: A Modern Life in Ancient Christian Orthodoxy.* New York: Putnam, 1999.

Milne, A. A. *Winnie-the-Pooh.* New York: Dutton, 1954.

Nouwen, Henri J., Donald P. McNeill, and Douglas A. Morrison. *Compassion: A Reflection on the Christian Life.* Garden City, N.Y.: Doubleday, 1982.

O'Connor, Flannery. *The Habit of Being: Letters of Flannery O'Connor.* Edited by Sally Fitzgerald. New York: Farrar, Straus and Giroux, 1979.

———. *Mystery and Manners.* New York: Farrar, Straus and Giroux, 1957.

Partnow, Elaine, ed. *The New Quotable Woman.* New York: Facts on File, 1992.

Peck, Scott M. *The Road Less Travelled: A New Psychology of Love, Traditional Values and Spiritual Growth.* New York: Touchstone, Simon and Schuster, 1978.

Potok, Chaim. *My Name Is Asher Lev.* New York: Fawcett Books, 1972.

Sawyer, Joy. *Dancing to the Heartbeat of Redemption: The Creative Process of Spiritual Growth.* Downers Grove, Ill.: InterVarsity, 2000.

Townsend, John. *Hiding from Love: How to Change the Withdrawal Patterns That Isolate and Imprison You.* Colorado Springs: NavPress, 1991.

Wangerin, Walter, Jr. *Ragman and Other Cries of Faith.* San Francisco: Harper and Row, 1984.

Welty, Eudora. *One Writer's Beginning.* Cambridge: Harvard University Press, 1984.

White, E.B. *Charlotte's Web.* New York: Harper, 1952.

Williams, Tennessee. "The Glass Menagerie." In *Six Great Modern Plays.* New York: Dell, 1956.

Yancey, Phillip, ed. *Reality and the Vision: Eighteen Contemporary Writers Tell Who They Read and Why.* Dallas: Word, 1990.

————. *What's So Amazing About Grace?* Grand Rapids, Mich.: Zondervan, 1997.